T0360512

Brands and Consumers

Brand management is firmly established as a core business and marketing activity. The research evidence on how consumers react to branding, however, is in constant evolution globally. This short-form book provides a comprehensive overview of research evidence on several core branding topics whilst acting as a catalyst for advancing future research and informing business practice.

The book fills a gap created by prior volumes on branding that, although well-illustrated and explained, have often approached the subject in somewhat uncritical manner. The book represents a timely compendium on popular topics in branding and aims to be a valuable addition to knowledge in branding. The book focuses on reviewing research in branding and brand management, and proposes areas for expanding research in the field. Recognising the diversity of research in branding, the authors of this book, as active branding researchers, attempt to discuss the limitations of current research and provide insights for future explorations.

The book will be of interest and a resource for academic researchers, branding practitioners, business students and policymakers who view branding as an evidence-oriented discipline.

Jaywant Singh is Professor of Marketing at Southampton Business School, University of Southampton, UK.

Benedetta Crisafulli is Senior Lecturer in Marketing at Birkbeck, University of London, UK.

State of the Art in Business Research

Series Editor: Geoffrey Wood

Recent advances in theory, methods and applied knowledge (alongside structural changes in the global economic ecosystem) have presented researchers with challenges in seeking to stay abreast of their fields and navigate new scholarly terrains.

State of the Art in Business Research presents shortform books which provide an expert map to guide readers through new and rapidly evolving areas of research. Each title will provide an overview of the area, a guide to the key literature and theories and time-saving summaries of how theory interacts with practice.

As a collection, these books provide a library of theoretical and conceptual insights, and exposure to novel research tools and applied knowledge, that aid and facilitate in defining the state of the art, as a foundation stone for a new generation of research.

Healthcare Management Control
A Research Overview
Michelle Carr and Matthias Beck

Comparative Corporate Governance
A Research Overview
Thomas Clarke

Brands and Consumers
A Research Overview
Jaywant Singh and Benedetta Crisafulli

For more information about this series, please visit: www.routledge. com/State-of-the-Art-in-Business-Research/book-series/START

Brands and Consumers

A Research Overview

Jaywant Singh and Benedetta Crisafulli

Routledge
Taylor & Francis Group

LONDON AND NEW YORK

First published 2023
by Routledge
4 Park Square, Milton Park, Abingdon, Oxon OX14 4RN

and by Routledge
605 Third Avenue, New York, NY 10158

Routledge is an imprint of the Taylor & Francis Group, an informa business

© 2023 Jaywant Singh and Benedetta Crisafulli

The right of Jaywant Singh and Benedetta Crisafulli to be identified as authors of this work has been asserted in accordance with sections 77 and 78 of the Copyright, Designs and Patents Act 1988.

British Library Cataloguing-in-Publication Data
A catalogue record for this book is available from the British Library

Library of Congress Cataloging-in-Publication Data
Names: Singh, Jaywant, author.
Title: Brands and consumers : a research overview / Jaywant Singh and Benedetta Crisafulli.
Description: 1 Edition. | New York, NY : Routledge, 2023. |
Series: State of the art in business research |
Includes bibliographical references and index.
Identifiers: LCCN 2022044994 (print) | LCCN 2022044995 (ebook)
Subjects: LCSH: Branding (Marketing)–Management. | Marketing research.
Classification: LCC HF5415.1255 .S5236 2023 (print) |
LCC HF5415.1255 (ebook) | DDC 658.8/27–dc23/eng/20220915
LC record available at https://lccn.loc.gov/2022044994
LC ebook record available at https://lccn.loc.gov/2022044995

ISBN: 978-1-138-32689-7 (hbk)
ISBN: 978-1-032-44330-0 (pbk)
ISBN: 978-0-429-44959-8 (ebk)

DOI: 10.4324/9780429449598

Typeset in Times New Roman
by Newgen Publishing UK

Contents

1 Introduction

The world is surrounded by a multitude of brands. There are brands for soft drinks, airlines, financial services, shower gel and even sport, cities and countries, and social networking sites. Despite the wide recognition that brands are important, defining what a brand stands for has been an issue open for debate in the past. De Chernatony and Dall'Olmo Riley (1998), for example, identified 12 types of brand definition. One of the most common is that a brand is a name, symbol, word or mark that identifies and distinguishes a proposition or company from its competitors. This definition is consistent with the one from the American Marketing Association (AMA) suggesting that a brand is "a name, term, design, symbol, or any other feature that identifies one seller's goods or service as distinct from those of other sellers" (2022a). While meaningful, this definition narrowly focuses on the identification of products through a brand. In this respect, Aaker (2014) observes that brands are "far more than a name or a logo … it is an organization's promise to a customer to deliver what a brand stands for … in terms of functional benefits but also emotional, self-expressive and social benefits" (p. 1). In other words, brands make promises to customers in a way that differentiates an offering from competing alternatives, while also delivering emotional or functional value to consumers.

While the original purpose of brands was to associate a brand to the owner and/or producer so that consumers would be aware and able to recognise an offering (identification), later advances have led managers to employ brands for the purpose of differentiation as well (Roper & Parker, 2006). Amid growing competition, a brand can benefit from awareness (identification), brand attitude and associations (differentiation) (Keller, 1998; Rossiter, 2014). Unlike early days when functional or rational attributes (e.g., size, packaging, quality, availability and price) were the basis of differentiation, non-functional, emotional differentiation is increasingly being communicated by brands

DOI: 10.4324/9780429449598-1

(Roper & Parker, 2006). Gradually, brands have also been recognised as a method of personification. As suggested by Aaker (1997), consumers ascribe dimensions of personality to brands just like they do with humans. Simultaneously, brands are seen as an asset, leading to increasing focus on brand equity, behavioural brand loyalty and brand choice measurement (Aaker, 1991; Jacoby & Chestnut, 1978).

As per the ISO brand standards, a brand is considered "an intangible asset" intended to create "distinctive images and associations in the minds of stakeholders, thereby generating economic benefit/value" (ISO 2020). A brand functions as the currency of products or services whose associations are meaningful to consumers, thus enjoy positive perceptions and feelings. As perceptions and feelings reside in the mind of consumers, consumers and brands are invariably intertwined. Even though marketing managers are responsible for creating, sustaining and nurturing the identity of brands, the meaning and value that consumers give to the brand are pivotal. The branding process, by which companies help consumers to differentiate between various offerings, equally involves both managers and consumers.

Brands represent opportunities for both consumers and organisations (e.g., manufacturers and retailers). It is therefore not surprising that *branding* has long been recognised as a core marketing activity. Thanks to branding, organisations buy and sell products and/or services easily, efficiently and relatively quickly. Furthermore, branding enables organisations to charge premium pricing, to increase the financial value of the company, and to deter new competitors from entering the market. When dealing with high equity brands, organisations also leverage on the opportunity to create brand extensions and brand alliances (Aaker, 1990; Rao et al., 1999; Singh et al., 2014). For consumers, brands remain essential tools as identifiers, guarantees and risk-reducers, whether purchasing fast-moving consumer goods or industrial products, in-store or online, and in industries such as sport, politics, arts, services and higher education. In addition, brands are thought to enable consumers to create meanings for themselves in the social world of consumption (Belk, 1988; Escalas & Bettman, 2005).

The study of brands and consumers has attracted notable interest among scholars for decades. Studies on consumers and brands are consistently published in a wide range of academic journals. Multiple streams of branding research have emerged over the years. A notable stream of work concerns consumer–brand relationships. Originally, brands were considered a merely strategic tool to facilitate selling. Unsurprisingly, early brand management research examined the role of the management team in the development of brand meaning.

Such a perspective implied that brands are 'owned' by organisations, which hold control over brand meaning (Boatwright et al., 2009). A subsequent body of scholarly research has recognised that brands are co-created with consumers (Vargo & Lusch, 2004). This has applications for the development of brand extensions (Boon et al., 2016) and/ or brand meaning, which has transitioned from being developed by companies – storytelling – to being developed by consumers – storygiving (Hughes et al., 2016). Such a novel perspective aligns with the growth of research on consumer engagement (Dessart et al., 2015; Hollebeek et al., 2014), brands and self-extension (Belk, 1988).

As the concept of consumer–brand relationships has taken shape, scholarly work on brand experiences has also emerged Brakus et al., 2009; O'Cass & Grace, 2004). As a relationship-oriented concept, brand experience holds relevance as consumers increasingly have multiple interactions with brands during the course of a relationship (Lemon & Verhoef, 2016). With technological advances, the concept of brand experience has extended to the online context, whether on social media or through the companies' websites. Literature on brand experience has prominently grown in service contexts, given the relationship-oriented nature of services (Dall'Olmo Riley & de Chernatony, 2000). An associated trend is illustrated by the increase in research on consumer associations and responses to brand alliances (also known as co-branding). Several aspects have been the focus of research on brand alliances, including perceived fit (Samuelsen et al., 2015), quality signalling (Rao et al., 1999), positive spillover effects of alliance information (Simonin & Ruth, 1998) and negative spillover (Votolato & Unnava, 2006), brand power in alliances (Kupfer et al., 2018) and brand equity effects (Kalafatis et al., 2012; Singh et al., 2019; Washburn et al., 2004).

With respect to the outcomes of branding, research has focused on measuring positive company outcomes. There is a noteworthy body of work investigating constructs such as brand love (Batra et al., 2012; Karjaluoto et al., 2016; Kaufmann et al., 2016), brand advocacy (Wallace et al., 2014), brand trust (Ha, 2004; Singh et al., 2022) and brand loyalty (Aksoy et al., 2014; Oliver, 1999). In a departure from the above, scholars have also focused on negative brand outcomes. In this regard, studies have examined information overload (Hutter et al., 2013), consumer responses to brand crises (Grappi et al., 2013; Singh et al., 2020) as well as negative reviews from other consumers (Allard et al., 2020).

An important novel development in marketing research concerns the focus on delivering offerings that add value not only to consumers and partners, but also to the wider society. An up-to-date definition of marketing by the AMA is that marketing represents "the activity, set of institutions and processes for creating, communicating, delivering and exchanging offerings that have value for customers, clients, partners, and society at large" (2022b). In line with the above paradigm shift, corporate social responsibility (CSR) is nowadays recognised as a field of study within the management and marketing disciplines (Lockett et al., 2006). Research on CSR and branding has spurred, following recognition that brands shall hold onto their responsibilities to society and engage in activities that contribute to social good. Scholarly attention to brands' CSR efforts and consequent consumer responses is on the rise, as evidenced by the number of publications and special issues on the topic in leading academic journals. Among other themes, branding research has addressed the role of consumers' ethical self-identity in relation to brands' CSR efforts (Singh, 2016), consumers' responses to CSR positioning of new brands (Robison & Wood, 2018), the effect of CSR on brands during times of recession (Bhattacharya et al., 2020) as well as CSR for luxury brands (Park et al., 2019) and job seekers' responses to brands' socially irresponsible actions (Antonetti et al., 2020). Furthermore, a stream of work expands on the conceptualisation of brands' socially responsible efforts, examining the concepts of doing well by doing good brand innovations (Varadarajan & Kaul, 2018), cause-related marketing (Singh et al., 2019; Vanhamme et al., 2012) and social innovation launch strategies in industrial markets (Crisafulli et al., 2020).

Branding research mostly consists of one-off studies which are meaningful for the purpose of advancing knowledge. However, such studies do not always establish generalisability of findings across contexts, countries and/or product categories. Given that generalisability is a cornerstone of scientific research, a substantial body of branding research supported by robust empirical evidence has focused on examining how people buy their brands. Spanning over six decades, this stream of work is based on real purchase data, often sourced from leading consumer panels such as GfK, Nielsen, Kantar and IRI. The seminal publications by Andrew Ehrenberg (e.g., Ehrenberg 1959, 1972, 1988; Ehrenberg et al., 2004) and colleagues (e.g., Singh et al., 2008) are considered a milestone in branding research with a behavioural perspective. The authors discovered patterns of buyer behaviour that are empirically generalised across a range of product categories, time period, countries and contexts. They established that consumers buy brands following largely habitual and law-like patterns (e.g., Ehrenberg et al., 1990; Sharp et al., 2012; Singh et al., 2012). Branding knowledge is enriched by the findings from this stream of research. Above all, the findings have direct applications in marketing practice and are employed in decision-making by a large number of companies around the world.

The abovementioned areas provide an overview of the impressive developments in scholarly research in branding, which continues to expand the boundaries of knowledge. Some of the new streams of work include research on Artificial Intelligence (AI) in marketing (Huang & Rust, 2021), the implications of AI for brand experiences (Kietzmann et al., 2018; Kumar et al., 2019), consumer–brand relationships (Cheng & Jiang, 2022) and brand buying behaviour (Sharp & Romaniuk, 2016). In addition, novel neuroscientific methods are being employed to understand consumer emotions and cognitions towards brands (Chan et al., 2018).

Multiple streams of branding research have therefore emerged over the past six decades or so. This book brings together key streams of branding research offering a source of knowledge for academic researchers and branding practitioners. The book presents an overview of research advances in key areas on the interface of branding and consumer research along with new perspectives in the domain. The book is a timely compendium on current issues in branding and brings together state-of-the-art literature in the domain. It is intended for postgraduate researchers, academics, branding specialists, marketers and brand managers looking for up-to-date evidence-based knowledge in branding. Given the array of research published in the area, this book provides an accessible roadmap for navigating through key streams of branding knowledge. In addition, it includes thought-provoking material on the future of brands and consumers, while providing a fertile ground of ideas for further branding research.

The book is comprised of seven chapters: (1) an overview on the evolution of branding research, (2) consumer–brand relationships, (3) brands and society, (4) brands in services, (5) how consumers buy brands, (6) brand partnerships and (7) new advances in branding research. The structure allows the exploration of knowledge in key areas of branding research, taking the reader through how novel thinking in branding has originated and evolved over time, the latest scholarly evidence and fruitful areas for further research. Below is a detailed overview of each chapter.

The introductory chapter (this chapter) presents the evolution of branding research, along with key domains in the study of brands and consumers. This chapter announces the dominant thinking and frameworks underlying the development of research in branding since the conception of branding as a topic and field of study. It highlights how various streams of work have developed and shaped our current thinking, while also explicating the diversity and richness of research in the area. The chapter concludes with the current outline of the book.

Chapter 2 focuses on how consumers relate to brands. Research on this topic has grown over the years in light of the recognition that consumers relate to brands just like they relate to humans, as part of their interpersonal relationships. The chapter introduces key branding constructs such as brand trust, commitment, love, engagement and brand-self connection, reviews the evidence on each and on the relationship between them. The chapter presents conclusions on the reviewed evidence and highlights areas for further research in the domain.

Chapter 3 addresses the role of brands in society. Research on CSR has exploded over the past few years. The chapter reviews scholarly evidence on how brands function in society, the impact of brands espousing social causes, brand activism and how consumers view such socially responsible initiatives, the larger role of brands in the society beyond profit motives. The chapter draws attention to some of the limitations of existing knowledge while suggesting fruitful areas for further research.

Chapter 4 reviews evidence on brands and consumers in service settings. Services contribute to a large proportion of the world's largest economies and have distinguishing features when compared with physical products. Branding plays a pivotal role in providing reassurance to consumers purchasing services, and in delivering enjoyable service experiences. The chapter addresses how service companies have turned into brands, explicates the concepts of service quality, satisfaction, service brand experience, service failure and recovery management and reviews related scholarly evidence. The chapter draws attention to the latest developments in service branding research and avenues for future enquiry.

Chapter 5 addresses the issues of how consumers buy their brands and the nature of brand loyalty. The focus is on a long-standing body of work on empirical generalisations in marketing concerning the measurement of brand performance and the prediction of brand purchase behaviour. The chapter includes a discussion of recent research advances and applications, and implications for future research.

Chapter 6 reviews scholarly evidence on brand partnerships. Brands often enter alliances in order to leverage on positive associations in consumers' mind and to launch new offerings in a cost-effective manner. The chapter includes a comprehensive explanation of the types of partnerships available to brands in B2C and B2B settings, and reviews evidence on the efficacy of alliances in engendering positive consumer responses. To conclude, the chapter presents areas worthy of further investigation.

Chapter 7 offers a review of novel approaches to brand–consumer research. Due to technological advances, marketing and branding are changing at a fast pace. The chapter discusses some of the most recent methodological advances in branding research, along with areas of work gaining rising scholarly attention. The chapter ends by presenting avenues for further research in this space.

References

Aaker, D. A. (1990). Brand extensions: The good, the bad, and the ugly. *Sloan Management Review*, *31*(4), 47–56.

Aaker, D. A. (1991). *Managing Brand Equity: Capitalizing on the Value of a Brand Name*. New York: The Free Press, Maxwell Macmillan International.

Aaker, D. A. (2014). *Aaker on Branding*. New York: Morgan James.

Aaker, J. L. (1997). Dimensions of brand personality. *Journal of Marketing Research*, *34*, 347–356.

Aksoy, L., Keiningham, T. L., & Oliver, R. L. (2014). Loyalty: Its Many Sources and Variations. In *Handbook of Service Marketing Research*, Rust, R. & Huang, M.-H. (eds.) Cheltenham: Edward Elgar Publishing (pp. 37–51).

Allard, T., Dunn, L. H., & White, K. (2020). Negative reviews, positive impact: Consumer empathetic responding to unfair word of mouth. *Journal of Marketing*, *84*(4), 86–108.

American Marketing Association. (2022a). Definitions of brand. Available at www.ama.org/the-definition-of-marketing-what-is-marketing/ (Accessed 15 August 2022).

American Marketing Association. (2022b). Marketing definitions. Available at www.ama.org/topics/marketing-definition/ (Accessed 28 August 2022).

Antonetti, P., Crisafulli, B., & Tuncdogan, A. (2020). "Just look the other way": Job seekers' reactions to the irresponsibility of market-dominant employers. *Journal of Business Ethics*, *174*, 403–422.

Batra, R., Ahuvia, A., & Bagozzi, R. P. (2012). Brand love. *Journal of Marketing*, *76*(2), 1–16.

Belk, R. (1988). Possessions and the extended self. *Journal of Consumer Research*, *15* (September), 139–168.

Bhattacharya, A., Good, V., & Sardashti, H. (2020). Doing good when times are bad: The impact of CSR on brands during recessions. *European Journal of Marketing*, *54*(9), 2049–2077.

Boatwright, P, Cagan, J., Kapur, D., & Saltiel, A. (2009). A step-by-step process to build valued brands. *Journal of Product & Brand Management*, *18*(1), 38–49.

Boon, E., Grant, P., & Kietzmann, J. (2016). Consumer generated brand extensions: Definition and response strategies. *Journal of Product & Brand Management*, *25*(4), 337–344.

Brakus, J. J., Schmitt, B. H., & Zarantonello, L. (2009). Brand experience: What is it? How is it measured? Does it affect loyalty? *Journal of Marketing*, *73*(3), 52–68.

Chan, H.-Y., Boksem, M., & Smidts, A. (2018). Neural profiling of brands: Mapping brand image in consumers' brains with visual templates. *Journal of Marketing Research*, August, *55*, 600–615.

Cheng, Y., & Jiang, H. (2022). Customer–brand relationship in the era of artificial intelligence: Understanding the role of chatbot marketing efforts. *Journal of Product & Brand Management*, *31*(2), 252–264.

Crisafulli, B., Dimitriu, R., & Singh, J. (2020). Joining hands for the greater good: Examining social innovation launch strategies in B2B settings. *Industrial Marketing Management*, *89*, 487–498.

Dall'Olmo Riley, F., & de Chernatony, L. (2000). The service brand as a relationship builder. *British Journal of Management*, *11*, 137–150.

de Chernatony, L., & Dall'Olmo Riley, F. (1998). Defining a brand: Beyond the literature with experts' interpretations. *Journal of Marketing Management*, *14*(4–5), 417–443.

Dessart, L., Veloutsou, C., & Morgan-Thomas, A. (2015). Consumer engagement in online brand communities: A social media perspective. *Journal of Product & Brand Management*, *24*(1), 28–42.

Ehrenberg, A. S. C. (1959). The pattern of consumer purchases. *Applied Statistics*, *8*, 26–41.

Ehrenberg, A. S. C. (1972/1988). *Repeat-Buying: Facts, Theory and Applications*, (1st and 2nd editions). London; Griffin; New York: Oxford University Press.

Ehrenberg, A. S. C., Goodhardt. G. J., & Barwise, P. (1990). Double jeopardy revisited. *Journal of Marketing*, *54*, 82–91.

Ehrenberg, A. S. C., Uncles, M. D., & Goodhardt, G. J. (2004). Understanding brand performance measures: Using Dirichlet benchmarks. *Journal of Business Research*, *57*(12), 1307–1325.

Escalas, J. E., & Bettman, J. R. (2005). Self-construal, reference groups, and brand meaning. *Journal of consumer research*, *32*(3), 378–389.

Grappi, S., Romani, S., & Bagozzi, R. P. (2013). The effects of company offshoring strategies on consumer responses. *Journal of the Academy of Marketing Science*, *41*(6), 683–704.

Ha, H-Y. (2004). Factors influencing consumer perceptions of brand trust online. *Journal of Product & Brand Management*, *13*(5), 329–342.

Hollebeek, L. D., Glynn, M. S., & Brodie, R. J. (2014). Consumer brand engagement in social media: Conceptualization, scale development and validation. *Journal of Interactive Marketing*, *28*(2), 149–165.

Huang, M.-H., & Rust, R. T. (2021). A strategic framework for artificial intelligence in marketing. *Journal of the Academy of Marketing Science*, *49*, 30–50.

Hughes, M., Bendoni, W. K., & Pehlivan, E. (2016). Storygiving as a co-creation tool for luxury brands in the age of the internet: A love story by Tiffany and thousands of lovers. *Journal of Product & Brand Management*, *25*(4), 357–364.

Hutter, K., Hautz, J., Dennhardt, S., & Füller, J. (2013). The impact of user interactions in social media on brand awareness and purchase intention: The case of MINI on Facebook. *Journal of Product & Brand Management*, *22*(5/6), 342–351.

ISO. (2020). What's in a brand? Quite a bit actually. Available at www.iso.org/ news/ref2486.html (Accessed 15 August 2022).

Jacoby, J., & Chestnut, R.W. (1978). *Brand Loyalty Measurement and Management*. New York: Wiley.

Kalafatis, S. P., Remizova, N., Riley, D., & Singh, J. (2012). The differential impact of brand equity on B2B co-branding. *Journal of Business & Industrial Marketing*, *27*(8), 623–634.

Karjaluoto, H., Munnukka, J., & Kiuru, K. (2016). Brand love and positive word of mouth: The moderating effects of experience and price. *Journal of Product & Brand Management*, *25*(6), 527–537.

Kaufmann, H. R., Loureiro, S. M. C., & Manarioti, A. (2016). Exploring behavioural branding, brand love and brand co-creation. *Journal of Product & Brand Management*, *25*(6), 516–526.

Keller, K. L. (1998). *Strategic Brand Management: Building, Measuring, and Managing Brand Equity*. Upper Saddle River, NJ: Prentice Hall.

Kietzmann, J., Paschen, J., & Treen, E. (2018). Artificial intelligence in advertising. How marketers can leverage artificial intelligence along the consumer journey. *Journal of Advertising Research*, *58*(3), 263–267.

Kumar, V., Rajan, B., Venkatesan, R., & Lecinski, J. (2019). Understanding the role of artificial intelligence in personalized engagement marketing. *California Management Review*, *61*(4), 135–155.

Kupfer, A.-K., vor der Holte, N. P., Kübler, R. V., & Hennig-Thurau, T. (2018). The role of the partner brand's social media power in brand alliances. *Journal of Marketing*, *82*(3), 25–44.

Lemon, K. N., & Verhoef, P. C. (2016). Understanding customer experience throughout the customer journey. *Journal of Marketing*, *80*(6), 69–96.

Lockett, A., Moon, J., & Visser, W. (2006). Corporate social responsibility in management research: Focus, nature, salience and sources of influence. *Journal of Management Studies*, *43*(1), 115–136.

O'Cass, A., & Grace, D. (2004). Exploring consumer experiences with a service brand. *Journal of Product & Brand Management*, *13*(4), 257–268.

Oliver, R. L. (1999). Whence consumer loyalty? *Journal of Marketing*, *63* (Special Issue), 33–44.

Park, J. K., Torelli, C. J., Monga, A. S. B., & John, D. R. (2019). Value instantiation: how to overcome the value conflict in promoting luxury brands with CSR initiatives. *Marketing Letters*, *30*, 307–319.

Rao, A. R., Qu, L., & Ruekert, R. W. (1999). Signaling unobservable product quality through a brand ally. *Journal of Marketing Research*, *36*(2), 258–268.

Robison, S., & Wood, S. (2018). A "good" new brand – What happens when new brands try to stand out through corporate social responsibility. *Journal of Business Research*, *92*, 231–241.

Roper, S., & Parker, C. (2006). Evolution of branding theory and its relevance to the independent retail sector. *Marketing Review*, *6*(1), 55–71.

Rossiter, J. R. (2014). Branding explained: Defining and measuring brand awareness and brand attitude. *Journal of Brand Management*, *21*(7–8), 533–540.

Samuelsen, B. M., Olsen, L. E., & Keller, K. L. (2015). The multiple roles of fit between brand alliance partners in alliance attitude formation. *Marketing Letters*, *26*, 619–629.

Sharp, B., & Romaniuk, J. (2016). *How Brands Grow*. Melbourne: Oxford University Press.

Sharp, B., Wright, M., Dawes, J., Driesener, C., Meyer-Waarden, L., Stocchi, L., & Stern, P. (2012). It's a Dirichlet world: Modeling individuals' loyalties reveals how brands compete, grow, and decline. *Journal of Advertising Research*, *52*(2), 203–213.

Simonin, B. L., & Ruth, J. A. (1998). Is a company known by the company it keeps? Assessing the spillover effects of brand alliances on consumer brand attitudes. *Journal of Marketing Research*, *35*(1), 30–42.

Singh, J. (2016). The influence of CSR and ethical self-identity in consumer evaluation of cobrands. *Journal of Business Ethics*, *138*(2), 311–326.

Singh, J., Crisafulli, B., Quamina, L. T., & Kottasz, R. (2019). The role of brand equity and crisis type on corporate brand alliances in crises. *European Management Review*, *17*(4), 821–834.

Singh, J., Crisafulli, B., & Xue, M. T. (2020). 'To trust or not to trust': The impact of social media influencers on the reputation of corporate brands in crisis. *Journal of Business Research*, *119*, 464–480.

Singh, J., Ehrenberg, A., & Goodhardt, G. (2008). Measuring customer loyalty to product variants. *International Journal of Market Research*, *50*(4), 513–532.

Singh, J., Kalafatis, S. P., & Ledden, L. (2014). Consumer perceptions of cobrands: the role of brand positioning strategies. *Marketing Intelligence & Planning*, *32*(2), 145–159.

Singh, J., Scriven, J., Clemente, M., Lomax, W., & Wright, M. (2012). New brand extensions: Patterns of success and failure. *Journal of Advertising Research*, *52*(2), 234–242.

Singh, J., Shukla, P., & Schlegelmilch, B. B. (2022). Desire, need, and obligation: Examining commitment to luxury brands in emerging markets. *International Business Review*, *31*(3), 101947.

Vanhamme, J., Lindgreen, A., Reast, J., & van Popering, N. (2012). To do well by doing good: Improving corporate image through cause-related marketing. *Journal of Business Ethics*, *109*, 259–274.

Varadarajan, R., & Kaul, R. (2018). Doing well by doing good innovations: Alleviation of social problems in emerging markets through corporate social innovations. *Journal of Business Research*, *86*, 225–233.

Vargo, S. L., & Lusch. R. F. (2004). Evolving to a new dominant logic for marketing. *Journal of Marketing*, *68*(1), 1–17.

Votolato, N. L., & Unnava, H. R. (2006). Spillover of negative information on brand alliances. *Journal of Consumer Psychology*, *16*(2), 196–202.

Wallace, E., Buil, I., & de Chernatony, L. (2014). Consumer engagement with selfexpressive brands: Brand love and WOM outcomes. *Journal of Product & Brand Management*, *23*(1), 33–42.

Washburn, J. H., Till, B. D., & Priluck, R. (2004). Brand alliance and customer-based brand-equity effects. *Psychology & Marketing*, *21*(7), 487–508.

2 Consumer–Brand Relationship

2.1 Introduction

The study of consumer–brand relationships represents a paradigm shift in marketing theory and research. Traditionally, marketing has been depicted as a one-directional interaction process wherein a product or service is sold to consumers. If successful, marketing would make consumers more receptive to marketed, branded offerings than commodity offerings. Presently, marketing entails a multi-stakeholder process where interaction is multidirectional, multidimensional and complex. Under the new paradigm of consumer–brand relationships, the role of brands as merely identifiers of products and services has undergone a transformation. A considerable body of research has investigated how building relationships enables companies to create greater consumer engagement, differentiation and loyalty (e.g., Bonchek & France, 2016; Dhaoui & Webster, 2021; Escalas & Bettman, 2005; Fournier, 1998). The concept of consumer–brand relationships has witnessed growing research attention since the 1990s. The trend has been accompanied by an emphasis on the study of emotions, and the development of emotion-focused constructs, such as brand passion, love and intimacy. Another stream of research has suggested that consumers relate to brands in the same way in which they relate to other humans, as part of their interpersonal relationships.

This chapter focuses on the foundations of the concept of consumer–brand relationships and related advances in marketing research. It reviews scholarly evidence in the domain, focusing on key relationship constructs such as brand trust, commitment, love, engagement and self-brand connection. The chapter reviews the evidence on each construct and the relationship between them. It draws conclusions on the reviewed evidence and highlights areas for further research in the domain.

DOI: 10.4324/9780429449598-2

2.2 The Foundations of the Concept of Consumer–Brand Relationships

The concept of consumer–brand relationships originates in the work of Fournier (1998). Fournier's work has influenced branding research, and the concept of branding as a result has broadened. As postulated in the seminal paper, Fournier (1998) explains that relationships have inspired studies in business markets, analysing how partnerships between suppliers and manufacturers are established (e.g., Dwyer et al., 1987; Sheth & Parvatiyar, 1995). Comparatively less attention has traditionally been directed towards understanding how consumers bond with brands, until the work of Fournier (1998). An exception is customer loyalty, which has a long research tradition. Notwithstanding its significance, the main criticism of studies on loyalty concerns the conceptualisation and operationalisation of relationships as being constrained to consumers' repeat purchase behaviour or inertia (Jacoby & Chestnut, 1978). Fournier (1998) proposed a renewed perspective on consumer–brand relationships grounded on the premise that brands are "animated, humanized, or somehow personalized" (p. 344). By anthropomorphising objects such as brands, interactions are facilitated and so is relationship-building. Consistent with this view, a stream of research on impression formation has developed on brands as intentional agents (e.g., Fournier & Alvarez, 2012), showing that human traits of competence and warmth are assigned to brands just as these are assigned to individuals (e.g., Kervyn et al., 2012). Likewise, communal and exchange norms of interpersonal relationships are shown to underpin relationships between brands and consumers (Aggarwal, 2004).

Research identifies several types of consumer–brand relationships. Some consumer–brand relationships resemble a friendship or even marriages, wherein commitment between the parties involved tends to be high and so might be affect (Fournier 1998). Other relationships present aspects of dependency and risk and/or are temporally oriented. In this sense, relationships do tend to vary and are grounded on different cognitions and/or emotions. Less strong relationships are more grounded in cognitive, rational judgements, such as judgement of risk. As posited by Fournier (1998), strong relationships are built on 'rich affective grounding' which is reminiscent of concepts of love, and reflect self-brand connection and interdependence. Several of the above contentions have been challenged by empirical evidence-based research by Ehrenberg, and more recently by Sharp and colleagues (see Chapter 5).

Investigating the drivers of consumer–brand relationships, research spawned a variety of relationship-focused concepts, including self-brand connections (e.g., Escalas & Bettman, 2005), brand attachment (e.g., Belaid & Temessek Behi, 2011), brand passion (e.g., Albert et al., 2008), brand commitment (e.g., Keiningham et al., 2015) and brand love (e.g., Batra et al., 2012). These novel branding concepts have impacted research in several domains, as discussed in Section 2.3.

2.3 Self-Brand Connection

Academic work on self-brand connection is twofold. One stream of literature builds on the work of Aaker (1997) on brand personality. The premise of such research is that brands have an identity, akin to a set of human characteristics (Aaker, 1997). Brands represent symbols whose meaning is employed to define a consumer's self-concept (Levy, 1959). This perspective borrows from a wealth of knowledge on consumer possessions demonstrating that possessions are used to satisfy psychological needs, including creating one's self-concept, reinforcing and expressing self-identity (e.g., Dwayne et al., 1992; Kleine et al., 1995). Extending research on possessions to branding, Escalas and Bettman (2013) demonstrate that consumers make brand choices based on the congruency between brand and self-image associations. Given the focus on how brands shape the self-concept, the measures of self-concept and brand image have traditionally been used to operationalise the link between brands and self-identity, though only a moderate effect could be found (Sirgy, 1982). This body of work recognises that reference groups are also a pivotal source of brand meanings. Consumers form beliefs about the world through observations of reference groups, thus groups with whom they share beliefs and similarity on various relevant characteristics. Consumer research has demonstrated an association between group membership and brand usage (e.g., Bearden & Etzel, 1982; Bearden et al., 1989). In this respect, Escalas and Bettman (2005) have shown that brands with images consistent with the ingroup enhance self-brand connections, while brands with images that are consistent with the outgroup have a negative effect on consumers.

A second stream of research builds on the assumption that not only brands have an identity, but consumers do as well. In this respect, a notable perspective on brands and the self is offered by a research tradition commonly known as Consumer Culture Theory (CCT). CCT is concerned with the ways in which consumers, through brands and marketing materials, forge a sense of the self (Arnould & Thompson, 2005; Belk, 1988). A fundamental premise of this body of work is that individuals construct narratives of identity when making choices and in playing their role in the marketplace (Belk, 1988; Levy, 1996). As best exemplified by Arnould and Thompson (2005), "consumers are conceived of as identity seekers and makers" (p. 871). Studies in this domain seek to explain the relationship between consumers' identity and the marketplace, positing that consumers often choose to inhabit marketplaces and embrace cultural scripts that align with their identity (Arnould & Thompson, 2005). For instance, Belk et al. (2003) show how the desire of consumers is channelled onto objects of consumption and is created by ideals propagated by discourses of corporate capitalism.

The work of Russell Belk on the theory of extended self is prominent in this research tradition. A fundamental tenet is that the self is defined and expressed by our choice of brands (Belk, 1988). As illustrated by Belk (1988), "we are what we have" (p. 160). In other words, consumers experience self-extension via the mastery of an object, the creation or knowledge of an object, and via habituation. For instance, the purchase of an autonomous car might define one's status as innovative. Likewise, the purchase of luxury clothing might invigorate one's impression and status to others in society. Consumers extend the self in the products they own and the individuals they count as family and friends (Belk, 1988). At times, consumers go as far as glorifying brands by making them possessions and extensions of the self (Belk et al., 1989). A notable example is the way in which consumers personalise products to make these theirs or display brand logos like the Nike swoosh to establish and convey their identity. Both experimental and interpretative studies provide empirical support for the link between the extended self and brand consumption (e.g., Mittal, 2006; Schouten & McAlexander, 1995). Prior evidence extends to both owned and not-yet-owned brands (Belk, 2013). The work recognises that the extended self does not only operate at the level of the individual, but also at a collective level which involves family, group and national identities (Belk, 1988). Consumers at a given time share a passion for the same products or brands, thus are part of an identity shared with others (Belk, 1988). Such identities have been captured in the concepts of brand communities (McAlexander et al., 2002; Muñiz & O'Guinn, 2001), brand tribes (Cova & Cova, 2001) and brand cults (Belk & Tumbat, 2005).

As evidenced in the earlier discussion, marketing scholars have been interested in exploring the relationship between brands and the self with the view to explain the components of such a relationship, and how intertwined these are. Research on brand identity is relatively well-established. There are, however, comparatively fewer studies on consumer identity and how it relates to brands, and specifically, on the interplay between consumer identity and brand identity. Studies have traditionally focused on strategic marketing questions concerning what marketing can do to shape brands in ways which are profitable to companies, yet overlooking what consumers can do to influence brands. This is a potentially fruitful area for further research. With the fast growth of products enabled by Artificial Intelligence including, for instance, autonomous cars and washing machines, or semi-autonomous vacuum cleaners, consumers often face a moral dilemma between adoption out of enhanced convenience and non-adoption due to the risks associated with lost control (e.g., lost control and foregone enjoyment of driving in the case of autonomous cars, see for instance Bonnefon et al., 2016). Future research could focus on the role played by identity in such brand choices.

2.4 Brand Engagement

The concept of engagement has been treated as a property of the brand, hence the term 'brand engagement', or as a feature of consumers, which explains the term 'consumer engagement'. The two concepts invariably overlap despite the different designations. As exemplified by Hollebeek et al. (2014), consumers, brands, offerings and organisations can all be key engagement objects. In practice, brand engagement has been the object of investigations depicting consumers as largely passive players in consumer–brand relationships. Gradually and particularly with the work of van Doorn et al. (2010) and Hollebeek (2011), there has been a shift in scholarly discourse towards recognising the active role played by consumers in brand-based processes (e.g., Hollebeek et al., 2014; Pagani et al., 2011). In contrast to established concepts that capture consumer–brand relationships, such as brand commitment, brand relationship quality, or brand involvement (Hollebeek, 2011), consumer engagement offers a revised view of relationships that is highly interactive (Hollebeek et al., 2014) and social (Vivek et al., 2012). Consumer engagement has therefore been seen as a construct that more explicitly accounts for consumers' interactive brand-related dynamics (Brodie et al., 2011), building on the tenets of CCT (Arnould & Thompson, 2005) and the service-dominant logic (Karpen et al., 2012; Vargo & Lusch 2004, 2008). According to CCT, consumers actively use marketplace ideologies and map their identity via brand meaning (Murray, 2002; Thompson & Haytko, 1997). The service-dominant logic postulates that consumers proactively participate towards creating personalised experiences by pursuing active interactions with companies (Vargo & Lusch, 2004; 2008). The two theoretical lenses complement one another in putting consumers at the centre of value creation and in describing their active role in interacting with brands (Leckie et al., 2016).

Following the above view, Brodie et al. (2011) suggest that "specific interactive experiences are an indispensable component of a customer's particular engaged state" and that such interactions take place between a specific "engagement subject" (e.g., consumer) and "engagement object" (e.g., brand or product) (p. 259). With the increased interest in understanding the active role of consumers and their interactive experience with brands, a scale of consumer brand engagement (CBE) has been developed by Hollebeek et al. (2014). The concept of CBE seeks to depart conceptually from the 'brand engagement in self-concept' scale developed by Sprott, Czellar and Spangenberg's (2009) to gauge "an individual difference representing consumers' propensity to include important brands as part of how they view themselves" (p. 92). The interactive experience of consumers with the brand is a distinctive feature of the CBE construct.

The marketing literature has since grown and spurred a variety of engagement-based concepts, generally separated into cognitive, affective and behavioural dimensions (Dhaoui & Webster, 2011). With the growth of the digital space, the concept of *online* consumer engagement has attracted significant scholarly attention (Baldus et al., 2015; Brodie et al., 2013; Dessart et al., 2016). For example, research examines social media engagement as manifested with incentivised referrals, social media conversations about products/brands and customer feedback to companies (Hughes et al., 2019). Likewise, consumer engagement with social media posts has been a topic of enquiry (e.g., Giakoumaki & Krepapa, 2020).

Research on consumer engagement is largely well-established. Notwithstanding, more work in this domain is warranted given the exponential growth of social media which have engagement at the very core. Prior research has largely focused on consumer engagement with brands (e.g., Dessart et al., 2016; Gambetti & Graffigna, 2010). In practice, engagement is inherently social and interactive. In social networks, for instance, consumers engage with other consumers. There is evidence that consumers engage with communities (Algesheimer et al., 2005), a social media post from other consumers (Giakoumaki & Krepapa, 2020) or social media influencers (Hughes et al., 2019). The focus so far has been on capturing engagement with one entity at a time, though consumers increasingly engage and enter into relationships with different entities simultaneously. Understanding the interplay between consumer engagement with the brand and engagement with other entities is an area of focus for future research. In addition, customer disengagement merits further empirical research.

2.5 Brand Trust, Brand Commitment and Brand Love

Originating in sociology (Becker, 1960), the concept of commitment gained footing in marketing research thanks to the work of Moorman et al. (1992) and Morgan and Hunt (1994) on business-to-business relationships. Moorman et al. (1992) define commitment as an "enduring desire to maintain a valued relationship" (p. 316). Such a definition of commitment is grounded on interorganisational relationships, typically based on mutual trust between the parties and the expected accomplishment of mutual benefits. Borrowing from this body of work, the concept of commitment has gradually been applied to explain consumer–brand relationships. In this domain, Gustafsson et al. (2005) refer to commitment as a form of 'stickiness' that "keeps consumers loyal to a brand or firm even when satisfaction may be low" (p. 211).

Commitment and trust have often been examined in tandem. As best exemplified by Morgan and Hunt (1994), trust implies confidence in the integrity and reliability of another party in the relationship. Trust has traditionally been seen as an antecedent to commitment. This is consistent with social exchange theory (Cropanzano & Mitchell, 2005) suggesting that relationships built on trust are valued to the extent that the parties desire to commit themselves towards maintaining the relationship. Trust has been studied in a variety of social exchange contexts. For instance, in communications, trust in the source of the message has been studied and commonly identified as source credibility. In services marketing, trust is seen as important towards encouraging customers to buy a service before experiencing it (Parasuraman et al., 1991). In strategic alliances and buyer–seller exchanges, trust is seen as a pivotal component of cooperative problem-solving (Schurr & Ozanne, 1985). While often conceptualised as an antecedent to commitment, brand trust has been measured as a predictor of commitment (Shukla et al., 2016) or as an indicator of affective commitment (Gustafsson et al., 2005). This implies that brand trust is often treated as a necessary condition for commitment to be exposed. While distinct from an operationalisation point of view, conceptually trust and commitment are not always distinct.

While originally proposed as a unidimensional construct (e.g., Moorman et al., 1992; Morgan & Hunt, 1994), there is nowadays scholarly consensus on the multidimensionality of commitment (e.g., Singh et al., 2022). Most studies refer to three main dimensions of commitment – affective, calculative and normative (Keiningham et al., 2015). Affective commitment entails a form of psychological attachment to the brand grounded on shared values and identification with the brand (Evanschitzky et al., 2006). Affective commitment has been linked to retention, brand repurchase, positive word of mouth and willingness to pay a price premium (Albert & Merunka, 2013). Calculative commitment represents a more rational, economic-based dependence on a brand, driven by the lack of alternatives or high switching costs that pose a challenge when seeking to end the relationship with the brand (Evanschitzky et al., 2006; Fullerton, 2005). Normative commitment denotes psychological attachment based on an individual sense of obligation to a relationship and to the brand (Jones et al., 2010). Social pressure, need for approval or motivation to comply with normative beliefs tend to define normative commitment (Jones et al., 2010; Larivière et al., 2014).

Among the three dimensions, affective commitment has often been studied and identified as a predictor of loyal behaviour. By encouraging the continuation of a relationship with the brand, commitment implies that consumers want to continue re-using, repurchasing and re-patronising the brand (Shuv-Ami, 2012). Further, commitment is found to act as a buffer in attenuating consumer response to negative information about the brand (Germann et al., 2014). It also increases consumer resistance to switching (Srivastava & Owens, 2010) and reduces the number of brands in consumers' consideration set (Raju & Unnava, 2006). In the context of luxury buying, affective commitment is found to encourage consumption satisfaction and advocacy intentions (Shukla et al., 2016). Recent evidence from cross-country data in China, India, Russia, Thailand and Turkey shows the pivotal role of affective commitment in driving consumer intentions to purchase luxury goods (Singh et al., 2022). While conceptually similar, consumer commitment differs from consumer loyalty. In fact, loyalty is often an outcome of brand trust and commitment, yet loyal behaviour such as repeat purchases may or may not be indicative of high commitment (Keiningham et al., 2015).

While trust and commitment imply a cognitive assessment of the benefits and risks of building and maintaining a relationship, brand love accounts for the emotional needs underpinning relationship building. A notable area for research enquiry in the field of consumer–brand relationships concerns brand love (Ahuvia, 2005; Albert & Merunka, 2013; Albert et al., 2008; Batra et al., 2012; Bergkvist & Bech-Larsen, 2010; Carroll & Ahuvia, 2006; Fournier, 1998). Brand love has been defined as a set of "cognitions, emotions, and behaviors, which consumers organize in a mental prototype" (Batra et al., 2012, p. 2). The work of Ahuvia (2005) is seminal in this respect demonstrating the role of beloved objects and activities in forming relationships with brands. Grounded in the theories of para-social love and interpersonal love (Batra et al., 2012; Langner et al., 2015), the construct of brand love has been regarded as comparable to humans' interpersonal love (Lastovicka & Sirianni, 2011). Similarities have been drawn between individuals' emotional feelings towards loved ones and the emotions held by consumers towards brands (Albert & Valette-Florence, 2010). Given its link to emotions, brand love has often been treated as overlapping with brand passion (e.g., Ahuvia et al., 2009; Albert et al., 2008; Batra et al., 2012) and emotional attachment, especially in hedonic product categories as opposed to utilitarian ones (Carroll & Ahuvia, 2006). The discriminant validity between the two overlapping concepts can therefore be questioned, and this invariably represents a limitation of research on brand love.

Among the outcomes of brand love, research associates the construct with a number of organisational benefits including brand loyalty (Park et al., 2006), positive word of mouth and brand advocacy (Batra et al., 2012). Another outcome of brand love relates to positive brand associations, which in turn predict affective commitment (Albert & Valette-Florence, 2010) and willingness to pay a premium price (Albert & Merunka, 2013). Brand love has also been linked to brand engagement. For instance, young consumers' love towards smartphones has been linked with brand engagement (Junaid et al., 2019).

Research on brand love has, however, not been short of criticisms. The idea that brand love can provide companies with a leverage against 'not loved' competitors is counter to empirical generalisations in marketing showing that most brands, even dominant most loved ones, have several light/infrequent buyers, as buyers rarely see anything special about the brands they purchase, even those that buyers claim to love (Romaniuk, 2013). Furthermore, the management approach of asking consumers to rate their love for a brand arguably presents some weaknesses given that, in the best-case scenario, likeability is the best proxy of love that can practically be captured, even when asking consumers about brands or sectors in which they have a genuine interest (Dawes, 2014). Such critiques are a timely reminder for circumspection towards popular constructs. Further empirical evidence from a behavioural perspective could help in establishing whether consumer love for brands is real or purely an academic construct with limited managerial relevance.

Altogether, brand trust, commitment and love have received considerable scholarly attention. Notwithstanding, the changing marketing landscape calls for the revisitation and/or expansion of the existing knowledge base. Nowadays, given the ubiquity of consumer choice, there could be less scope for brands to build and maintain affective commitment. This is in contrast with the opportunity to foster calculative commitment. With the advances in technology allowing brands to build personalised relationships with consumers, calculative commitment could be taking the centre stage. In this sense, consumers might envisage the benefits of enjoying personalised relationships offered by the brand as highly enticing regardless of whether they have any affective disposition towards the brand. Further research in this direction is needed. Likewise, despite the popularity of brand love among brand managers, distinguishing brand love from other proximal constructs such as brand liking (Langner et al., 2015; Sternberg, 1986), brand passion (Carroll & Ahuvia, 2006) or brand attachment (Park et al., 2006; Park et al., 2010) appears still challenging. Further studies could address this issue explicitly.

Finally, research examining the negative emotions in consumer–brand relationships is constrained to a handful of studies. In a literature review on the topic, Khatoon and Rheman (2021) note that evidence on the subject is limited and addresses only certain discrete negative emotions, including hate (Curina et al., 2020; Fetscherin, 2019; Hegner et al., 2017; Kucuk, 2019), anger (Beverland et al., 2010; Mende et al., 2019), fear (Hille et al., 2015; Kordrostami & Kordrostami, 2019) and disappointment (Guèvremont & Grohmann, 2013; Huber et al., 2010). In practice, as highlighted in the discussion in Chapter 4 on brands in services, emotions are an important component in the appraisal of negative events with the brand, especially when a consumer–brand relationship already exists, and consumers might feel betrayed. Furthermore, emotion theory suggests that consumers often experience emotional ambivalence (Andrade & Cohen, 2007). For instance, consumers might experience positive emotions about the brand but negative emotions towards the prospect of entering a long-term relationship they might not be able to exit at a later stage. Further research is needed to identify instances of emotional ambivalence, the psychological mechanisms employed by consumers to resolve such conflicting emotions and the behavioural consequences with respect to the relationship with the brand.

References

Aaker, J. (1997). Dimensions of brand personality. *Journal of Marketing Research, 34* (August), 347–357.

Aggarwal, P. (2004). The effects of brand relationship norms on consumer attitudes and behavior. *Journal of Consumer Research, 31*(1), 87–101.

Ahuvia, A. C. (2005). Beyond the extended self: Loved objects and consumers' identity narratives. *Journal of Consumer Research*, *32*(1), 171–184.

Ahuvia, A. C., Batra, R., & Bagozzi, R. P. (2009). Love, Desire, and Identity: A Conditional Integration Theory of the Love of Things. In *Handbook of Brand Relationships*, MacInnis, D. J., Park, C. W., & Priester, J. W. (Eds.). New York: Routledge.

Albert, N., & Merunka, D. (2013). The role of brand love in consumer–brand relationships. *Journal of Consumer Marketing*, *30*(3), 258–266.

Albert, N., Merunka, D., & Valette-Florence, P. (2008). When consumers love their brands: Exploring the concept and its dimensions. *Journal of Business Research*, *61*(10), 1062–1075.

Albert, N., & Valette-Florence, P. (2010). Measuring the love feeling for a brand using interpersonal love items. *Journal of Marketing Development and Competitiveness*, *5*(1), 57–63.

Algesheimer, R., Dholakia, U. M., & Herrmann, A. (2005). The social influence of brand community: Evidence from European car clubs. *Journal of Marketing*, *69*(3), 19–34.

Andrade, E. B., & Cohen, J. B. (2007). On the consumption of negative feelings. *Journal of Consumer Research*, *34*(3), 283–300.

Arnould, E. J., & Thompson, C. J. (2005). Consumer culture theory (CCT): Twenty years of research. *Journal of Consumer Research*, *31*(4), 868–882.

Baldus, B. J., Voorhees, C., & Calantone, R. (2015). Online brand community engagement: Scale development and validation. *Journal of Business Research*, *68*(5), 978–985.

Batra, R., Ahuvia, A., & Bagozzi, R. P. (2012). Brand love. *Journal of Marketing*, *76*(2), 1–16.

Bearden, W. O., & Etzel, M. J. (1982). Reference group influence on product and brand purchase decisions. *Journal of Consumer Research, 9*(September), 183–194.

Bearden, W. O., Netemeyer, R. G., & Etzel, M. J. (1989). Measurement of consumer susceptibility to inter-personal influence. *Journal of Consumer Research, 15*(March), 473–481.

Becker, H. S. (1960). Notes on the concept of commitment. *American Journal of Sociology*, *66*(1), 32–40.

Belaid, S. & Temessek Behi, A. (2011). The role of attachment in building consumer–brand relationships: An empirical investigation in the utilitarian consumption context. *Journal of Product & Brand Management*, *20*(1), 37–47.

Belk, R. W. (1988). Possessions and the extended self. *Journal of Consumer Research, 15*(September), 139–168.

Belk, R. W. (2013). Extended self in a digital world. *Journal of Consumer Research*, *40*(October), 477–500.

Belk, R. W., Ger, G., & Askegaard, S. (2003). The fire of desire: A multisited inquiry into consumer passion. *Journal of Consumer Research, 30*(3), 326–351.

Belk, R. W., & Tumbat, G. (2005). The cult of Macintosh. *Consumption, Markets and Culture, 8* (September), 205–218.

Belk, R. W., Wallendorf, M., & Sherry Jr., J. F. (1989). The sacred and the profane in consumer behavior: Theodicy on the odyssey. *Journal of Consumer Research*, *16*(1), 1–38.

Bergkvist, L., & Bech-Larsen, T. (2010). Two studies of consequences and actionable antecedents of brand love. *Journal of Brand Management*, *17*(7), 504–518.

Beverland, M. B., Kates, S. M., Lindgreen, A., & Chung, E. (2010). Exploring consumer conflict management in service encounters. *Journal of the Academy of Marketing Science*, *38*(5), 617–633.

Bonchek, M., & France, C. (2016). Build your brand as a relationship. *HBR. org*. Available at https://hbr.org/2016/05/build-your-brand-as-a-relationship (Accessed 10 August 2022).

Bonnefon, J.-F., A. Shariff, & Rahwan I. (2016). The social dilemma of autonomous vehicles. *Science, 352*, 1573–1576.

Brodie, R. J., Hollebeek, L. D., Juric, B., & Ilic, A. (2011). Customer engagement: Conceptual domain, fundamental propositions & implications for research in service marketing. *Journal of Service Research*, *14*(3), 252–271.

Brodie, R. J., Ilic, A., Juric, B., & Hollebeek, L. D. (2013). Consumer engagement in a virtual brand community: An exploratory analysis. *Journal of Business Research*, *66*(1), 105–114.

Carroll, B. A., & Ahuvia, A. C. (2006). Some antecedents and outcomes of brand love. *Marketing Letters*, *17*(2), 79–89.

Cova, B., & Cova, V. (2001). Tribal marketing: The tribalization of society and its impact on the conduct of marketing. *European Journal of Marketing*, *36*(5/6), 595–620.

Cropanzano, R., & Mitchell, M. S. (2005). Social exchange theory: An interdisciplinary review. *Journal of Management*, *31*(6), 874–900.

Curina, I., Francioni, B., Hegner, S. M., & Cioppi, M. (2020). Brand hate and non-repurchase intention: A service context perspective in a cross-channel setting. *Journal of Retailing and Consumer Services*, *54*, 102031.

Dawes, J. (2014). 'Brand Love'– Another misleading and distracting idea that professional marketers should avoid. Available at SSRN: https://ssrn.com/abstract=2425044

Dessart, L., Veloutsou, C., & Morgan-Thomas, A. (2016). Capturing consumer engagement: Duality, dimensionality and measurement. *Journal of Marketing Management*, *32*(5/6), 399–426.

Dhaoui, C., & Webster, C. M. (2021). Brand and consumer engagement behaviors on Facebook brand pages: Let's have a (positive) conversation. *International Journal of Research in Marketing*, *38*, 155–175.

Dwayne Ball, A. & Tasaki, L. H. (1992). The role and measurement of attachment in consumer behavior. *Journal of Consumer Psychology*, *1*(2), 155–172.

Dwyer, F. R., Schurr, P. H., & Oh, S. (1987). Developing buyer–seller relationships. *Journal of Marketing*, *51*(2), 11–27.

Escalas, J. E., & Bettman, J. R. (2005). Self-construal, reference groups, and brand meaning. *Journal of Consumer Research*, *32*(3), 378–389.

Escalas, J. E., & Bettman, J. R. (2013). The Brand Is 'Me': Exploring the Effect of Self-Brand Connections on Processing Brand Information as Self Information. In *The Routledge Companion to Identity and Consumption*, Ruvio, A. & Belk, R. (Eds.). London: Routledge (pp. 366–378).

Evanschitzky, H., Iyer, G. R., Plassmann, H., Niessing, J., & Meffert, H. (2006). The relative strength of affective commitment in securing loyalty in service relationships. *Journal of Business Research, 59*(12), 1207–1213.

Fetscherin, M. (2019). The five types of brand hate: How they affect consumer behavior. *Journal of Business Research, 101*, 116–127.

Fournier, S. (1998). Consumers and their brands: Developing relationship theory in consumer research. *Journal of Consumer Research, 24*, 343–373.

Fournier, S., & Alvarez, C. (2012). Brands as relationship partners: Warmth, competence, and in-between. *Journal of Consumer Psychology, 22*(2), 177–185.

Fullerton, G. (2005). How commitment both enables and undermines marketing relationships. *European Journal of Marketing, 39*(11/12), 1372–1388.

Gambetti, R. C., & Graffigna, G. (2010). The concept of engagement: A systematic analysis of the ongoing marketing debate. *International Journal of Market Research, 52*, 801–826.

Germann, F., Grewal, R., Ross, W. T., & Srivastava, R. K. (2014). Product recalls and the moderating role of brand commitment. *Marketing Letters, 25*(2), 179–191.

Giakoumaki, C., & Krepapa, A. (2020). Brand engagement in self-concept and consumer engagement in social media: The role of the source. *Psychology & Marketing, 37*(3), 457–465.

Guèvremont, A., & Grohmann, B. (2013). The impact of brand personality on consumer responses to persuasion attempts. *Journal of Brand Management, 20*(6), 518–530.

Gustafsson, A., Johnson, M. D., & Roos, I. (2005). The effects of customer satisfaction, relationship commitment dimensions, and triggers on customer retention. *Journal of Marketing, 69*(October), 210–218.

Hegner, S. M., Fetscherin, M., & van Delzen, M. (2017). Determinants and outcomes of brand hate. *Journal of Product and Brand Management, 26*(1), 13–25.

Hille, P., Walsh, G., & Cleveland, M. (2015). Consumer fear of online identity theft: Scale development and validation. *Journal of Interactive Marketing, 30*, 1–19.

Hollebeek, L. (2011). Exploring customer brand engagement: Definition and themes. *Journal of Strategic Marketing, 19*(7), 555–573.

Hollebeek, L. D., Glynn, M. S., & Brodie, R. J. (2014). Consumer brand engagement in social media: Conceptualization, scale development and validation. *Journal of Interactive Marketing, 28*(2), 149–165.

Huber, F., Vollhardt, K., Matthes, I., & Vogel, J. (2010). Brand misconduct: Consequences on consumer–brand relationships. *Journal of Business Research, 63*(11), 1113–1120.

Hughes, C., Swaminathan, V., & Brooks, G. (2019). Driving brand engagement through online social influencers: An empirical investigation of sponsored blogging campaigns. *Journal of Marketing*, *83*(5), 78–96.

Jacoby, J., & Chestnut, R.W. (1978). *Brand Loyalty Measurement and Management*. New York: Wiley.

Jones, T., Fox, G. L., Taylor, S. F., & Fabrigar, L. R. (2010). Service customer commitment and response. *Journal of Services Marketing*, *24*(1), 16–28.

Junaid, M., Hou, F., Hussain, K., & Kirmani, A. A. (2019). Brand love: The emotional bridge between experience and engagement, generation-M perspective. *Journal of Product & Brand Management*, *28*(2), 200–215.

Karpen, I. O., Bove, L. L., & Lukas, B. A. (2012). Linking service-dominant logic and strategic business practice: A conceptual model of a service-dominant orientation. *Journal of Service Research*, *15*(1), 21–38.

Keiningham, T. L., Frennea, C. M., Aksoy, L., Buoye, A., & Mittal, V. (2015). A five component customer commitment model: Implications for repurchase intentions in goods and services industries. *Journal of Service Research*, *18*(4), 433–450.

Kervyn, N., Fiske, S. T., & Malone, C. (2012). Brands as intentional agents framework: How perceived intentions and ability can map brand perception. *Journal of Consumer Psychology*, *22*(2), 166–176.

Khatoon, S., & Rehman, V. (2021). Negative emotions in consumer brand relationship: A review and future research agenda. *International Journal of Consumer Studies*, *45*(4), 719–749.

Kleine, S. S., Kleine III, R. E., & Allen, C. T. (1995). How is a possession 'Me' or 'Not Me'? Characterizing types and an antecedent of material possession attachment. *Journal of Consumer Research*, *22*(December), 327–343.

Kordrostami, M., & Kordrostami, E. (2019). Secure or fearful, who will be more resentful? Investigating the interaction between regulatory focus and attachment style. *Journal of Product and Brand Management*, *28*(5), 671–683.

Kucuk, S. U. (2019). Consumer brand hate: Steam rolling whatever I see. *Psychology & Marketing*, *36*(5), 431–443.

Langner, T., Schmidt, J., & Fischer, A. (2015). Is it really love? A comparative investigation of the emotional nature of brand and interpersonal love. *Psychology & Marketing*, *32*(6), 624–634.

Larivière, B., Keiningham, T. L., Cooil, B., Aksoy, L., & Malthouse, E. C. (2014). A longitudinal examination of customer commitment and loyalty. *Journal of Service Management*, *25*(1), 75–100.

Lastovicka, J. L., & Sirianni, N. J. (2011). Truly, madly, deeply: Consumers in the throes of material possession love. *Journal of Consumer Research*, *38*(2), 323–342.

Leckie, C., Nyadzayo, M. W., & Johnson, L. W. (2016). Antecedents of consumer brand engagement and brand loyalty. *Journal of Marketing Management*, *32*(5/6), 558–578.

Levy, S. J. (1959). Symbols for sale. *Harvard Business Review*, *37*(July–August), 117–124.

Levy, S. J. (1996). Stalking the wild amphisbaena. *Journal of Consumer Research*, *23*(December), 163–176.

McAlexander, J. H., Schouten, J.W., & Koening, H. J. (2002). Building brand community. *Journal of Marketing*, *66*(January), 38–54.

Mende, M., Scott, M. L., Garvey, A. M., & Bolton, L. E. (2019). The marketing of love: How attachment styles affect romantic consumption journeys. *Journal of the Academy of Marketing Science*, *47*(2), 255–273.

Mittal, B. (2006). I, Me, Mine – How products become consumers' extended selves. *Journal of Consumer Behaviour*, *5*, 550–562.

Moorman, C., Zaltman, G., & Deshpande, R. (1992). Relationships between providers and users of market research: The dynamics of trust within and between organizations. *Journal of Marketing Research*, *29*(3), 314–328.

Morgan, R. M., & Hunt, S. D. (1994). The commitment-trust theory of relationship marketing. *Journal of Marketing*, *58*(3), 20–38.

Muñiz, A. M., Jr., & O'Guinn, T. C. (2001). Brand community. *Journal of Consumer Research*, *27*(4), 412–432.

Murray, J. B. (2002). The politics of consumption: A re-inquiry on Thompson and Haytko's (1997) "Speaking of Fashion". *Journal of Consumer Research*, *29*, 427–440.

Pagani, M., Hofacker, C. F., & Goldsmith, R. E. (2011). The influence of personality on active and passive use of social networking sites. *Psychology & Marketing*, *28*(5), 441–456.

Parasuraman, A., Berry, L. L., & Zeithaml, V. A. (1991). Understanding customer expectations of service. *Sloan Management Review*, *32*(3), 39–48.

Park, C. W., MacInnis, D. J., & Priester, J. R. (2006). Beyond attitudes: Attachment and consumer behavior. *Seoul National Journal*, *12*(2), 3–36.

Park, C. W., MacInnis, D. J., Priester, J. R., Eisingerich, A. B., & Iacobucci, D. (2010). Brand attachment and brand attitude strength: Conceptual and empirical differentiation of two critical brand equity drivers. *Journal of Marketing*, *74*(6), 1–17.

Raju, S., & Unnava, R. H. (2006). The mediating role of arousal in brand commitment. *Advances in Consumer Research*, *33*, 517–519.

Romaniuk, J. (2013). Viewpoint. What's (brand) love got to do with it? *International Journal of Market Research*, *55*(2), 185–186.

Schouten, J., & McAlexander, J. (1995). Subcultures of consumption: An ethnography of the new biker. *Journal of Consumer Research*, *22*(June), 43–62.

Schurr, P. H., & Ozanne, J. L. (1985). Influences on exchange processes: Buyers' preconceptions of a seller's trustworthiness and bargaining toughness. *Journal of Consumer Research*, *11*(4), 939–953.

Sheth, J. N., & Parvatiyar, A. (1995). The evolution of relationship marketing. *International Business Review*, *4*(4), 397–418.

Shukla, P., Banerjee, M. & Singh, J. (2016). Customer commitment to luxury brands: Antecedents and consequences. *Journal of Business Research*, *69*, 323–331.

Shuv-Ami, A. (2012). Brand commitment: A new four-dimensional (4 Es) conceptualisation and scale. *Journal of Customer Behaviour*, *11*(3), 281–305.

Singh, J., Shukla, P., & Schlegelmilch, B. B. (2022). Desire, need, and obligation: Examining commitment to luxury brands in emerging markets. *International Business Review, 31*(3)101947.

Sirgy, J. (1982). Self-concept in consumer behavior: A critical review. *Journal of Consumer Research, 9*(December), 287–300.

Sprott, D., Czellar, S., & Spangenberg, E. (2009). The importance of a general measure of brand engagement on market behavior: Development and validation of a scale. *Journal of Marketing Research, 46*(1), 92–104.

Srivastava, P., & Owens, D. L. (2010). Personality traits and their effect on brand commitment: An empirical investigation. *Journal of Marketing Management, 20*(2), 15–27.

Sternberg, R. J. (1986). A triangular theory of love. *Psychological Review, 93*(2), 119–135.

Thompson, C. J., & Haytko, D. L. (1997). Speaking of fashion: Consumers' uses of fashion discourses and the appropriation of countervailing cultural meanings. *Journal of Consumer Research, 24*, 15–42.

van Doorn, J., Lemon, K. N., Mittal, V., Nass, S., Peck, D., Pirner, P., & Verhoef, P. C. (2010). Customer engagement behavior: Theoretical foundations and research directions. *Journal of Service Research, 13*(3), 253–266.

Vargo, S. L., & Lusch. R. F. (2004). Evolving to a new dominant logic for marketing. *Journal of Marketing, 68*(1), 1–17.

Vargo, S. L., & Lusch. R. F. (2008). Service-dominant logic: Continuing the evolution. *Journal of the Academy of Marketing Science, 36*(1), 1–10.

Vivek, S., Beatty, S. E., & Morgan, R. (2012). Customer engagement: Exploring customer relationships beyond purchase. *Journal of Marketing Theory & Practice, 20*(2), 122–146.

3 Brands and Society

3.1 Introduction

There has been a substantial mindset shift since the economist Milton Friedman's assertion that the sole purpose of businesses is to generate profits. Businesses are nowadays playing a proactive role in supporting the society. Consumers are more aware of brands' social responsibilities, and their expectations are shaping branding strategies. Crucially, consumers view themselves as playing a role in creating social and environmental changes and are often willing to participate in a brand's socially responsible efforts. There are a variety of ways in which brands engage with consumers and vice versa thanks to the digital media. Consumer awareness and media sophistication are also creating fresh challenges for brands in terms of engaging consumers in socially responsible practices and seeking novel approaches towards brand communication.

In scholarly research, studies on social cause marketing, for example, have advanced understanding on brands' relationship with the society. Even the learned bodies, such as the American Marketing Association, have included societal responsibility in their updated definition of marketing. In the business domain, the Business Roundtable – an influential group of corporate leaders – drawing upon the notion of 'conscious capitalism', have redefined the purpose of the company as having a broader responsibility to society that can be best addressed by considering all stakeholders in society when it comes to business decisions.[1] In practice, several global corporations, such as Unilever, embrace social purpose and sustainable living at the core of their branding strategy. 'Brand with a purpose' for the society has emerged as the pivotal leitmotif for brands. On the other hand, consumer scepticism about businesses partaking in societal welfare remains undiminished, presenting an ongoing challenge for the researchers and branding practitioners.

DOI: 10.4324/9780429449598-3

This chapter focuses on the latest developments in research on the changing ecosystem in which brands and consumers are entering a symbiotic relationship. The chapter reviews key research on how brands function in a societal setting, the business impact of brands espousing social causes and how consumers view such socially responsible initiatives, along with the larger role of brands in the society, above and beyond profit motives. The chapter highlights the limitations in current knowledge and suggests directions for future researchers.

The way companies conduct their business has become the focus of increased public scrutiny. Brands are involved in several types of activities such as corporate social responsibility (CSR), cause-related marketing (CrM), brand activism and social innovations (SIs). Each activity has received considerable scholarly attention over the years and has led to continued public debates about brands' role in societal welfare. Below is a review of key research developments.

3.2 CSR and Brands

A commonly accepted conceptualisation for CSR concerns the business practice of going beyond legal obligations and a company's own interests to address and manage the impact that business activities have on society and the environment (Matten & Moon, 2008; McWilliams & Siegel, 2001; Van Marrewijk, 2003). CSR is about how companies, and their managers, interact with stakeholders, namely "persons or groups that have, or claim, ownership, rights, or interests in a corporation and its activities, past, present, or future" (Clarkson, 1995, p. 106), including consumers, suppliers, employees, investors and communities, as well as the natural environment (Bhattacharya et al., 2009).

Following some initial uncertainty around whether CSR provides returns to brands, several studies have shown that consumers like sustainable initiatives and report intentions to purchase brands they perceive to be socially responsible (e.g., Brown & Dacin, 1997; Chernev & Blair, 2015; Sen & Bhattacharya 2001; Trudel & Cotte, 2009). Consumers also display attitudinal loyalty towards CSR-minded brands (e.g., Homburg et al., 2013) and generate positive word-of-mouth (e.g., Du et al., 2011; Lacey et al., 2015). In addition, research shows that CSR can, under certain circumstances, offer a buffer against negative publicity and detrimental outcomes to brands facing a corporate crisis (e.g., Antonetti et al., 2021; Bolton & Mattila, 2015; Joireman et al., 2015; Klein & Dawar, 2004). In a review of the CSR literature, Sen et al. (2016) point to the fact that CSR can engender a range of

perceptions and behaviour that favour the brand, driven by both consumers' CSR-related motivations (e.g., consumer–company identification, affective motives) and their CSR-influenced product perceptions.
In a topical study, Bhattacharya et al. (2020) show the effect of CSR on
brands during times of recession. The findings demonstrate that CSR
initiatives during recessions are associated with increased perceptions
of brand value, and CSR initiatives such as charitable contributions
provide a signal to consumers of higher brand quality. Overall, there is
scholarly consensus about a range of benefits for the brands supporting
CSR activities.

In spite of the abovementioned well-established CSR benefits for the
brands, a critical question pertains to whether the CSR initiatives deliver
the promised societal good. Brands' intention to 'do good' is frequently
communicated in their CSR communication, which has become integral
to their branding strategy, and is portrayed in reports, press releases,
website and public relations. Apart from sporadic studies, however, the
ever-growing body of CSR literature offers little evidence of the tangible impact of CSR initiatives on society. For instance, some studies
have examined environmental outcomes, such as changes in toxic (Li
& Zhou, 2017) and carbon emissions (Wright & Nyberg, 2017), social
innovations (Crisafulli et al., 2020; Mithani, 2017), green innovations
(Lampikoski et al., 2014), diversity and gender equality (Nie et al.,
2018). An exception is Sinha and Chaudhari (2018) who show the positive impact of a CSR program that developed special classes for weaker
students. Similarly, Luo et al. (2018) show the positive impact of corporate philanthropy on tackling oil spills.

The above studies, however, do not lead to causal inferences about
the actual impact of the CSR initiative analysed. Barnett et al. (2020), in
their literature review and extensive analysis of thousands of studies on
CSR–performance claim that there is not a single study that adequately
demonstrates that CSR initiatives resolve the social problems which
they intended to address. The same authors suggest that the CSR field
should reconceive itself as a 'science of design' in which researchers
formulate initiatives that seek to achieve specific social and environmental objectives (see also Simon, 1988). Known as the behavioural
design approach, it has resonance with the studies in development economics (e.g., Banerjee & Duflo, 2009; Duflo et al., 2007). In the domain
of development economics, an 'evaluation revolution' employing field-
based randomised controlled trials has enabled the measurement of the
impact of a given program or policy, which in turn assists in designing
programs with high success potential (Datta & Mullainathan, 2014).
Similar approaches could provide a useful contribution to the body of

literature on how brands' CSR initiatives bring about the intended societal changes.

In addition to the interest in societal benefits accruing from brands' CSR initiatives, a substantial number of consumers, activists and academics believe that often brands benefit from *insincere* claims of CSR (Pope & Wæraas, 2016). The process of inferring the intentions of corporates is explained by attributions theory (Heider, 1958) postulating that people seek to understand the causes behind events and individual actions. Evidence from CSR literature suggests that consumers make attributions about the reason why companies engage in CSR and the likely motives behind socially responsible efforts (e.g., Du et al., 2010; Ellen et al., 2006; Yoon et al., 2006). Unlike attributions of genuine, other-focused motives, which are favourable to companies, attributions of egoistic and insincere motives pose an obstacle to the communication of CSR activities of the brand (Du et al., 2010). Consumers' attributions, therefore, influence the extent to which CSR efforts are likely to be effective or backfire.

The expression 'CSR-washing' has become part of the parlance, and in turn has influenced perceptions towards brands and their marketing campaigns (Kanter, 2009). Scholarly research has looked into the practice of CSR-washing, with studies asserting that false CSR claims are 'everywhere' (Alves, 2009; Delmas & Burbano, 2011; Lyon & Montgomery, 2013; Nyilasy et al., 2014). Others have claimed that such perceptions dissuade consumers from buying CSR products and discourage companies from participating in the CSR movement, both practices likely to be counterproductive to the society (e.g., Mayser & Zick 1993; Parguel et al. 2011; Wagner et al., 2009). Underlying the above discussion is a general sense of distrust and cynicism affecting consumers when evaluating the CSR activities of brands.

In a departure from the impetus on the effects of CSR-washing in scholarly debate, a literature review by Pope and Wæraas (2016) suggests that the phenomenon might not be as prevalent as suggested by several academic studies. The authors put forth that the perceptions of CSR-washing are highly contingent, complex and perhaps rare. Their main reasoning is that successful CSR-washing requires the alignment of nearly a half-dozen, highly contingent conditions. The authors maintain that

> "even if the condition were true that firms tend to decouple CSR statements from practices, such firms still could not successfully CSR-wash if their CSR advertisements did not reach consumers, if consumers could readily verify actual corporate practices, if consumers dismissed the CSR advertisements, if the competition

exposed the false advertisements, or if consumers, simply, did not highly value CSR."

(p. 186)

Such counter evidence against the prevailing belief on CSR scepticism, even though rare, presents a new perspective and merits consideration by future researchers. The United Nations' launch of the sustainable development goals (SDGs) and the Global Compact[7] initiative has added to the debate, especially when a large number of brands have embraced the SDGs in their corporate missions, raising the prospect of further stakeholder scepticism.

3.3 When Brands Employ Cause-Related Marketing

An increasingly popular branding strategy focusing on the society is Cause-related Marketing (CrM). In a CrM campaign, the brand supports a social cause when consumers contribute to product revenue (Barone et al., 2000; Varadarajan & Menon, 1988). With a CrM campaign, the brand aims to benefit directly in terms of increased sales while a small share of the generated revenue is directed towards supporting an important social cause such as donating water or medicines in countries in need. CrM has emerged as an appealing strategic tool in comparison to the general approach of CSR for the brands, for addressing both social and profit goals (Galan-Ladero et al., 2015; Lafferty et al., 2004). CrM has been shown to address the social, economic and environmental demand from the local stakeholders (Demetriou et al., 2010). Similarly, supporting social causes through CrM campaigns has been shown to benefit global brands in enhancing legitimacy and accountability when operating in a foreign country (Scherer & Palazzo, 2011), and the strategy is useful for building a desirable image and generating consumer support (Kostova et al., 2008). Over the past three decades, a substantial body of literature has examined CrM, its types, benefits and impact on consumer perceptions (e.g., Christofi et al., 2020; He et al., 2019; Koschate-Fischer et al., 2012; Robinson et al., 2012; Singh et al., 2020). In addition, a growing body of research is acknowledging the role of CrM as a viable business tool that can enhance a brand's sales performance and corporate reputation, and that may serve as a potential source of sustainable competitive advantage (e.g., Duarte & Silva, 2020; Larson et al., 2008; Liu, 2013).

Although CrM has been extensively researched, there are several areas that can be explored further. In a review of the related literature, Thomas et al. (2020) point to a dearth of research on the post-implementation effect of CrM. Similar to CSR more generally, studies focusing on the measurement of the impact of CrM programmes on society would further enrich knowledge on the viability of such a strategy. This is an important area to investigate that could help to assess whether CrM objectives are met and how CrM can be efficient for societal welfare. In another review of CrM literature in international marketing, Vrontis et al. (2020) highlight the need for further research on CrM in cross-cultural settings. The authors call for international marketing studies that focus on the value of CrM for global brands' competitiveness.

In this regard, an important issue concerns the use of emotional appeals in CrM communication. Kim and Johnson (2013), for example, suggest that the influence of ego-focused (vs. other-focused) emotions is greater for individualistic (vs collectivistic) consumers. An area for future research concerns how the *intensity* of these emotions in marketing communications influence consumer perceptions towards CrM across cultures, following the study by Singh et al. (2020) who examine the differential impact of guilt appeal intensity in CrM. Another area that merits research relates to the role of consumers' cognitive style in shaping responses to CrM across cultures. Although explored in general consumer research (e.g., Monga & John, 2007; 2010), cognitive style has not been investigated in the context of CrM. Cognitive styles determine the psychological processes individuals go through when seeking a causal explanation of events (Nisbett et al., 2001). For example, interdependent (similar to collectivism) consumers are more likely to use contextual information to draw inferences for the CrM campaign of a brand. Independent (or, individualistic) consumers, on the other hand, focus more on the attributes of the CrM cause–brand partnership. In particular, the cultural implication of cognition may unveil some fruitful findings with respect to the way CrM influences consumers across cultures (e.g., Ji & Yap, 2016; Markus & Kitayama, 1991). Temporal orientations are another area that has been overlooked in cross-cultural CrM research. A key issue in creating a CrM campaign is the temporal framing of the communication messages (e.g., Tangari et al., 2010). Given that consumers across cultures have a divergent temporal orientation (short-term oriented vs. long-term oriented), they might respond to CrM messages that feature various temporal durations differently. Further research could investigate the likely congruence between CrM messages and consumers' temporal orientation and belief systems.

The current state of research in CrM suggests a highly productive and uniform stream of papers in journals across the spectrum. Several theories from social and experimental psychology have been used to understand CrM and consumer behavior. The theories frequently employed by researchers are attribution theory, persuasion knowledge, altruism, congruence (e.g., brand-cause fit), warm-glow feeling, associative learning theory, the theory of reasoned action, signalling theory and self-construal theory. The main strands of investigation are around the impact of CrM on consumer perceptions, consumer purchase intentions, and evaluation of the firm and its motives using the above theories. Bergqvist and Zhou (2019) suggest that the new studies show incremental research, and include new variables, which indicates a relatively 'safe' approach. The authors make a valid point about future research taking a less safe route and expanding the boundaries of knowledge in CrM by employing new methodologies, theories and research approaches. Given the continuing popularity of CrM and its philanthropic aims of benefitting the society, the domain is well-disposed for exploring new avenues of research.

3.4 Brand Activism and Its Impact

Historically, brands have been averse to courting debatable and sometimes even contentious issues. An exception is the case, for instance, of the Italian brand Benetton espousing social causes such as AIDS prevention, same-sex relationships, capital punishment and racial equality in the eighties and the nineties. Over the past decade, however, there has been a slow but noticeable shift in practice. Many brands have actively entered political debates and appear less reluctant to take a public stance on important social issues. Such brands are termed 'woke' in the social media driven discourses. Defined as brand activism or corporate socio-political activism (CSA), the tactic is being embraced by a growing number of small and large brands (e.g., Bhagwat et al., 2020; Mirzaei et al., 2022; Moorman, 2020). Several recent public movements, such as the Me Too and Black Lives Matter campaigns, and other social issues pertaining to gun control, refugees, immigration, gender and racial equality, have been endorsed and publicised by brands through social media campaigns. Studies have found the positive impact of corporate political activism on firm performance (e.g., Hydock et al., 2020; Lux et al., 2011).

In light of the recent vocal socio-political stance adopted by several big brands, the topic has seen a renewed scholarly interest from a branding perspective. For instance, Vredenburg et al. (2020) make a distinction between authentic and inauthentic brand activism, and show that when brands match activist messaging, purpose, and values, with prosocial corporate practice, they engage in authentic brand activism, leading to positive brand perceptions. In contrast, a mismatch between messaging and the brand's corporate values leads to inauthentic brand activism and negative perceptions of 'woke washing'. Taking the issue of 'woke washing' further, Mirzaei et al. (2022) show that woke activism by the brands encourages consumer backlash as virtue-signalling efforts are perceived as inauthentic. The authors propose several dimensions within a woke branding authenticity framework. Further, highlighting the negative outcomes of CSA, Bhagwat et al. (2020) show that CSA elicits an adverse reaction from the investors who believe that such activities signal a distraction away from a firm's profit-oriented objectives, and towards a risky activity with uncertain outcomes.

In another recent work, Mukherjee and Althuizen (2020) show that consumers' disagreement with a brand's stand leads to the weakening of brand attitudes. The authors find that when consumers perceive incongruence between the brand and the taken stand on controversial socio-political issues, the negative impact of brand activism is weaker as consumers morally decouple the brand. In marketing practice, despite the high-profile instances of brand activism, it is often the bigger brands that are prone to taking a stance, as suggested in a commentary by Moorman (2020). Through a survey of marketing leaders, the same authors have found that only half of the surveyed managers show a risk-taking attitude and consider the practice of changing product offerings in response to political issues as apposite.

The above research advances demonstrate growing scholarly interest in understanding the facets of brand activism and their impact on the business and consumers. Given its nascent stage, so far, the focus of extant research has been mainly on the impact of CSA on consumers and other external stakeholders. Future research can examine the longevity of brand activism and its long-term societal impact. Social movements are at times short-lived, and once the media storm settles, there is little reckoning of the impact. Understanding the broader impact of a brand's stance in shaping public opinion and societal consciousness about the socio-political issue represents a rich area for future research. Another interesting area for further research concerns the influence of political orientation of consumers in their support or neglect of brands taking a stance for a social issue. For instance, a pertinent question regarding the abortion laws in the United States is – are the democrats more likely to support brands that take a stance on abortion than the republicans? The issue could be investigated with the lens of social dominance orientation originating in domain of political psychology (e.g., Ho et al., 2012; Pratto et al., 1994). Further, often the follow-up of a brand's advocacy and pronouncements of engagement in a social issue is not accounted for. For example, there is little publicly available information about the results of Starbucks' announcement in 2017 that the company would employ 10,000 refugees worldwide within five years. Impact evaluation studies can shed light on the effectiveness of brand activism, and help brands to combat negative perceptions of woke washing.

3.5　Brands Innovating for Social Good

Brands today aspire to integrate the sustainability agenda in their strategic vision. Spurred by the SDGs set out by the United Nations, growing consumer expectations, and technological advancements, businesses are increasingly directing attention towards creating innovative products and services that can benefit society. Sustainability-focused innovations or SIs are gaining impetus and increasingly appear high on companies' CSR programs. The literature in CSR uses various terminology to delineate SIs, thought these are at times overlapping in scope. Among others, there are 'sustainable innovations', 'ecological innovations' and 'environmental innovations' (Varadarajan, 2017). In practice, SIs pertain to offerings that are sustainable due to the lowered impact on the environment, or society, or specific social groups or all of these factors combined. SIs represent opportunities for businesses to innovate at a profit, while also solving problems or unmet needs of the society (Kanter, 1999). Such opportunities can be exploited by means of launching a new offering, introducing new processes or innovative practices that benefit the society, while providing economic and other benefits to for-profit brands (Varadarajan & Kaul, 2018). SIs now span across sectors such as technology, education, employment, energy and involve processes such as recycling sustainably, creating energy-efficient processes, waste management, humanitarian aid and safe drinking water provision.

Extant research on SIs addresses a variety of marketing issues through various theoretical lenses. For instance, research examines innovation-based sustainability strategies at the level of the organisation, focusing on key marketing capabilities required for such innovations (Mariadoss et al., 2011), and the implications of integrating an environmental specialist in a new product team for firm performance (Ebru & Di Benedetto, 2015). Research at the level of individual consumers addresses the positive effect of sustainable offerings, which involves a warm-glow effect accruing from firm's benevolence and results in a reduction in perceived purchase risk (Bhattacharya et al.,

2021). Other research in the domain explains the positive effect of green product virtue on consumer emotions and purchase intent (Spielmann, 2020), the effect of green product choice on enhanced enjoyment at the time of consumption (Tezer & Bodur, 2020) and the negative impact of sustainability attributes on consumers' preferences (Luchs et al., 2010).

Branding research, more specifically, has highlighted the importance of innovation as a driver of sustainability-enhancing business practices (e.g., Adams et al., 2016; Gupta & Kumar, 2013; Homburg et al., 2013; Nidumolu et al., 2009). Recent literature reviews by Foroudi et al. (2021), Dionisio and de Vargas (2020) and White et al. (2019) bring together studies on SIs and suggest several areas for further research. Future studies can adopt a branding viewpoint to examine the themes and contributions reflected in the existing SI literature. For instance, studies examining how the established branding constructs such as commitment, trust, image and corporate identity influence SI-driven branding strategy, could reveal new insights. Given the cross-disciplinary nature of extant SI research, it has the potential to bring rich insights into the branding domain. For instance, the impact of adopting the SI approach on brand's performance, attitudinal and behavioural outcomes can be compared vis-à-vis CSR- or CrM-driven branding strategies. There is an abundance of conceptual papers in SIs (e.g., Herrera, 2015; Tabares, 2020); this can provide a fertile ground for the development of branding-oriented research.

A viable area for future research pertains to SIs developed and launched through a social alliance, or a partnership between non-profits and for-profit brands. Social alliances involve at least one non-profit partner, and in addition to the traditional economic objectives, include non-economic objectives, that is, objectives that focus on improving social welfare (Berger et al., 2004). The economic objectives include a marketing objective for the brand and a fund-raising objective for the non-profits, creating a win-win strategy for both partners. In a notable empirical study, Crisafulli et al. (2020) demonstrate that a for-profit brand preparing to launch a social innovation (e.g., a new product for business buyers made of 75% recycled components) can seek to ally with either a non-profit (e.g., a non-profit promoting recycling) or a for-profit capable of SI (e.g., a for-profit commercialising recycled products). Both the non-profit and for-profit partners contribute to an SI purpose (e.g., selling computers made of 75% recycled material). If launched by an alliance, SIs lead to greater buyers' purchase intentions than SIs launched via an independent venture pursued by the for-profit brand alone. Future research could advance the novel idea of SI-based non-profit and for-profit alliances by examining the impact on the allied brands, the effectiveness of brand communications and attributions of intent.

Notes

1 https://qz.com/work/1690439/new-business-roundtable-statement-on-the-purpose-of-companies/
2 www.unglobalcompact.org

References

Adams, R., Jeanrenaud, S., Bessant, J., Denyer, D., & Overy, P. (2016). Sustainability oriented innovation: A systematic review. *International Journal of Management Reviews, 18*(2), 180–205.

Alves, I. M. (2009). Green spin everywhere: How greenwashing reveals the limits of the CSR paradigm. *Governance (An International Journal of Policy and Administration), II*(1), 1–26.

Antonetti, P., Crisafulli, B., & Tuncdogan, A. (2021). "Just look the other way": Job seekers' reactions to the irresponsibility of market-dominant employers. *Journal of Business Ethics, 174*(2), 403–422.

Banerjee, A. V., & Duflo, E. (2009). The experimental approach to development economics. *Annual Review of Economics, 1*(1), 151–178.

Barnett, M. L., Henriques, I., & Husted, B. W. (2020). Beyond good intentions: Designing CSR initiatives for greater social impact. *Journal of Management, 46*(6), 937–964.

Barone, M. J., Miyazaki, A. D., & Taylor, K. A. (2000). The influence of cause-related marketing on consumer choice: Does one good turn deserve another? *Journal of the Academy of Marketing Science, 28*(2), 248–262.

Berger, I. E., Cunningham, P. H., & Drumwright, M. E. (2004). Social alliances: Company/nonprofit collaboration. *California Management Review, 47*(1), 58–90.

Bergkvist, L., & Zhou, K. Q. (2019). Cause-related marketing persuasion research: An integrated framework and directions for further research. *International Journal of Advertising, 38*(1), 5–25.

Bhagwat, Y., Warren, N. L., Beck, J. T., & Watson IV, G. F. (2020). Corporate sociopolitical activism and firm value. *Journal of Marketing, 84*(5), 1–21.

Bhattacharya, A., Good, V., & Sardashti, H. (2020). Doing good when times are bad: The impact of CSR on brands during recessions. *European Journal of Marketing, 54*(9), 2049–2077.

Bhattacharya, C. B., Good, V., Sardashti, H., & Peloza, J. (2021). Beyond warm glow: The risk-mitigating effect of corporate social responsibility (CSR). *Journal of Business Ethics, 171*(2), 317–336.

Bhattacharya, C. B., Korschun, D., & Sen, S. (2009). Strengthening stakeholder–company relationships through mutually beneficial corporate social responsibility initiatives. *Journal of Business Ethics, 85*(2), 257–272.

Bolton, L. E., & Mattila, A. S. (2015). How does corporate social responsibility affect consumer response to service failure in buyer–seller relationships? Journal of Retailing, 91(1), 140−153.

Brown, T. J., & Dacin, P. (1997). The company and the product: Corporate beliefs and consumer product responses. *Journal of Marketing*, 61(1), 68−84.

Chernev, A. & Blair, S. (2015). Doing well by doing good: The benevolent halo of corporate social responsibility. *Journal of Consumer Research*, 41, 1412–1425.

Christofi, M., Vrontis, D., Leonidou, E., & Thrassou, A. (2020). Customer engagement through choice in cause-related marketing: A potential for global competitiveness. *International Marketing Review*, 37(4), 621–650.

Clarkson M. (1995). A stakeholder framework for analyzing and evaluating corporate social performance. *Academy of Management Review*, 20(1), 92–117.

Crisafulli, B., Dimitriu, R., & Singh, J. (2020). Joining hands for the greater good: Examining social innovation launch strategies in B2B settings. *Industrial Marketing Management*, 89, 487–498.

Datta, S., & Mullainathan, S. (2014). Behavioral design: A new approach to development policy. *Review of Income and Wealth*, 60(1), 7–35.

Delmas, M. A., & Burbano, V. C. (2011). The drivers of greenwashing. *California Management Review*, 54(1), 64–87.

Demetriou, M., Papasolomou, I., & Vrontis, D. (2010). Cause-related marketing: Building the corporate image while supporting worthwhile causes. *Journal of Brand Management*, 17(4), 266–278.

Dionisio, M., & de Vargas, E. R. (2020). Corporate social innovation: A systematic literature review. *International Business Review*, 29(2), 101641.

Du, S., Bhattacharya, C. B., & Sen, S. (2010). Maximizing business returns to corporate social responsibility (CSR): The role of CSR communication. *International Journal of Management Reviews*, 12(1), 9–19.

Du, S., Bhattacharya, C. B., & Sen, S. (2011). Corporate social responsibility and competitive advantage: Overcoming the trust barrier. *Management Science*, 57(9), 1528–1545.

Duarte, P. A. & Silva, S. C. (2020). The role of consumer-cause identification and attitude in the intention to purchase cause-related products. *International Marketing Review*, 37(4), 603–620.

Duflo, E., Glennerster, R., & Kremer, M. (2007). Using randomization in development economics research: A toolkit. *Handbook of Development Economics*, 4, 3895–3962.

Ebru, G. & Di Benedetto, C. A. (2015). Cross-functional integration in the sustainable new product development process: The role of the environmental specialist. *Industrial Marketing Management*, 50, 150–161.

Ellen, P. S., Webb, D. J., & Mohr, L. A. (2006). Building corporate associations: Consumer attributions for corporate socially responsible program. *Journal of the Academy of Marketing Science*, 34(2), 147–157.

Foroudi, P., Akarsu, T. N., Marvi, R., & Balakrishnan, J. (2021). Intellectual evolution of social innovation: A bibliometric analysis and avenues for future research trends. *Industrial Marketing Management*, 93, 446–465.

Galan Ladero, M. M., Galera Casquet, C., & Singh, J. (2015). Understanding factors influencing consumer attitudes toward cause-related marketing. *International Journal of Nonprofit and Voluntary Sector Marketing*, *20*(1), 52–70.

Gupta, S., & Kumar, V. (2013). Sustainability as corporate culture of a brand for superior performance. *Journal of World Business*, *48*(3), 311–320.

He, H., Chao, M. M., & Zhu, W. (2019). Cause-related marketing and employee engagement: The roles of admiration, implicit morality beliefs, and moral identity. *Journal of Business Research*, *95*, 83–92.

Heider, F. (1958). *The Psychology of Interpersonal Relations*. New York: Wiley.

Herrera, M. E. B. (2015). Creating competitive advantage by institutionalizing corporate social innovation. *Journal of Business Research*, *68*(7), 1468–1474.

Ho, A. K., Sidanius, J., Pratto, F., Levin, S., Thomsen, L., Kteily, N., & Sheehy-Skeffington, J. (2012). Social dominance orientation: Revisiting the structure and function of a variable predicting social and political attitudes. *Personality and Social Psychology Bulletin*, *38*(5), 583–606.

Homburg, C., Stierl, M., & Bornemann, T. (2013). Corporate social responsibility in business-to-business markets: How organizational consumers account for supplier corporate social responsibility engagement. *Journal of Marketing*, *77*(6), 54–72.

Hydock, C., Paharia, N., & Blair, S. (2020). Should your brand pick a side? How market share determines the impact of corporate political advocacy. *Journal of Marketing Research*, *57*(6), 1135–1151.

Ji, L. J., & Yap, S. (2016). Culture and cognition. *Current Opinion in Psychology*, *8*, 105–111.

Joireman, J., Smith, D., Liu, R. L., & Arthurs, J. (2015). It's all good: Corporate social responsibility reduces negative and promotes positive responses to service failures among value-aligned consumers. *Journal of Public Policy & Marketing*, *34*(1), 32–49.

Kanter, R. (1999), From spare change to real change: The social sector as beta site for business Innovation. *Harvard Business Review*, *77*(3), 122–132.

Kanter, J. (2009). Study: For consumers, green is greenwash. *The New York Times*, pp. 4–8. Available at http://green.blogs.nytimes.com/2009/04/30/study-for-consumers-green-is-greenwash/ (Accessed 18 August 2022).

Kim, J. E., & Johnson, K. K. (2013). The impact of moral emotions on cause-related marketing campaigns: A cross-cultural examination. *Journal of Business Ethics*, *112*(1), 79–90.

Klein, J., & Dawar, N. (2004). Corporate social responsibility and consumers' attributions and brand evaluations in a product–harm crisis. *International Journal of Research in Marketing*, *21*(3), 203–217.

Koschate-Fischer, N., Stefan, I. V., & Hoyer, W. D. (2012). Willingness to pay for cause-related marketing: The impact of donation amount and moderating effects. *Journal of Marketing Research*, *49*(6), 910–927.

Kostova, T., Roth, K., & Dacin, M. T. (2008). Institutional theory in the study of multinational corporations: A critique and new directions. *Academy of Management Review*, *33*(4), 994–1006.

Lacey, R., Kennett-Hensel, P. A., & Manolis, C. (2015). Is corporate social responsibility a motivator or hygiene factor? Insights into its bivalent nature. *Journal of the Academy of Marketing Science*, *43*(3), 315–332.

Lafferty, B. A., Goldsmith, R. E., & Hult, G. T. M. (2004). The impact of the alliance on the partners: A look at cause–brand alliances. *Psychology & Marketing*, *21*(7), 509–531.

Lampikoski, T., Westerlund, M., Rajala, R., & Möller, K. (2014). Green innovation games: Value-creation strategies for corporate sustainability. *California Management Review*, *57*(1), 88–116.

Larson, B. V., Flaherty, K. E., Zablah, A. R., Brown, T. J., & Wiener, J. L. (2008). Linking cause-related marketing to sales force responses and performance in a direct selling context. *Journal of the Academy of Marketing Science*, *36*(2), 271–277.

Li, X., & Zhou, Y. M. (2017). Offshoring pollution while offshoring production? *Strategic Management Journal*, *38*(11), 2310–2329.

Liu, G. (2013). Impacts of instrumental versus relational centered logic on cause-related marketing decision making. *Journal of Business Ethics*, *113*(2), 243–263.

Luchs, M. G., Naylor, R. W., Irwin, J. R., & Raghunathan, R. (2010). The sustainability liability: Potential negative effects of ethicality on product preference. *Journal of Marketing*, *74*(5), 18–31.

Luo, J., Kaul, A., & Seo, H. (2018). Winning us with trifles: Adverse selection in the use of philanthropy as insurance. *Strategic Management Journal*, *39*(10), 2591–2617.

Lux, S., Crook, T. R., & Woehr, D. J. (2011). Mixing business with politics: A meta-analysis of the antecedents and outcomes of corporate political activity. *Journal of Management*, *37*(1), 223–247.

Lyon, T. P., & Montgomery, A. W. (2013). Tweetjacked: The impact of social media on corporate greenwash. *Journal of Business Ethics*, *118*(4), 747–757.

Mariadoss, B. J., Tansuhaj, P. S., & Mouri, N. (2011). Marketing capabilities and innovation-based strategies for environmental sustainability: An exploratory investigation of B2B firms. *Industrial Marketing Management*, *40*(8), 1305–1318.

Markus, H. R., & Kitayama, S. (1991). Culture and the self: Implications for cognition, emotion, and motivation. *Psychological Review*, *98*(2), 224.

Matten, D., & Moon, J. (2008). "Implicit" and "explicit" CSR: A conceptual framework for a comparative understanding of corporate social responsibility. *Academy of Management Review*, *33*(2), 404–424.

Mayser, R. N., & Zick, C. D. (1993). Poisoning the well: Do environmental claims strain consumer credulity? *Advances in Consumer Research*, *20*(1), 698–703.

McWilliams, A. & Siegel, D. (2001). Corporate social responsibility: A theory of the firm perspective. *Academy of Management Review, 26*(1), 117–227.

Mirzaei, A., Wilkie, D. C., & Siuki, H. (2022). Woke brand activism authenticity or the lack of it. *Journal of Business Research, 139*, 1–12.

Mithani, M. A. (2017). Innovation and CSR—Do they go well together? *Long Range Planning, 50*(6), 699–711.

Monga, A. B., & John, D. R. (2007). Cultural differences in brand extension evaluation: The influence of analytic versus holistic thinking. *Journal of Consumer Research, 33*(4), 529–536.

Monga, A. B., & John, D. R. (2010). What makes brands elastic? The influence of brand concept and styles of thinking on brand extension evaluation. *Journal of Marketing, 74*(3), 80–92.

Moorman, C. (2020). Commentary: Brand activism in a political world. *Journal of Public Policy & Marketing, 39*(4), 388–392.

Mukherjee, S., & Althuizen, N. (2020). Brand activism: Does courting controversy help or hurt a brand? *International Journal of Research in Marketing, 37*(4), 772–788.

Nidumolu, R., Prahalad, C. K., & Rangaswami, M. R. (2009). Why sustainability is now the key driver of innovation. *Harvard Business Review, 82*(September), 57–67.

Nie, D., Lämsä, A. M., & Pučėtaitė, R. (2018). Effects of responsible human resource management practices on female employees' turnover intentions. *Business Ethics: A European Review, 27*(1), 29–41.

Nisbett, R. E., Peng, K., Choi, I., & Norenzayan, A. (2001). Culture and systems of thought: Holistic versus analytic cognition. *Psychological Review, 108*(2), 291.

Nyilasy, G., Gangadharbatla, H., & Paladino, A. (2014). Perceived greenwashing: The interactive effects of green advertising and corporate environmental performance on consumer reactions. *Journal of Business Ethics, 125*(4), 693–707.

Parguel, B., Benoît-Moreau, F., & Larceneux, F. (2011). How sustainability ratings might deter "greenwashing": A closer look at ethical corporate communication. *Journal of Business Ethics, 102*(1), 15–28.

Pope, S., & Wæraas, A. (2016). CSR-washing is rare: A conceptual framework, literature review, and critique. *Journal of Business Ethics, 137*(1), 173–193.

Pratto, F., Sidanius, J., Stallworth, L. M., & Malle, B. F. (1994). Social dominance orientation: A personality variable predicting social and political attitudes. *Journal of Personality and Social Psychology, 67*(4), 741.

Robinson, S. R., Irmak, C., & Jayachandran, S. (2012). Choice of cause in cause-related marketing. *Journal of Marketing, 76*(4), 126–139.

Scherer, A. G., & Palazzo, G. (2011). The new political role of business in a globalized world: A review of a new perspective on CSR and its implications for the firm, governance, and democracy. *Journal of Management Studies, 48*(4), 899–931.

Sen, S. & Bhattacharya, C.B. (2001). Does doing good always lead to doing better? Consumer reactions to corporate social responsibility. *Journal of Marketing Research*, *38*, 225–243.

Sen, S., Du, S., & Bhattacharya, C. B. (2016). Corporate social responsibility: A consumer psychology perspective. *Current Opinion in Psychology*, *10*, 70–75.

Simon, H. A. (1988). The science of design: Creating the artificial. *Design Issues*, *4*(1–2) 67–82.

Singh, J., Crisafulli, B., & Quamina, L. (2020). How intensity of cause-related marketing guilt appeals influences consumers: The roles of company motive and consumer identification with the brand. *Journal of Advertising Research*, *60*(2), 148–162.

Sinha, S. N. & Chaudhari, T. (2018). Impact of CSR on learning outcomes. *Management of Environmental Quality*, *29*(6), 1026–1041.

Spielmann, N. (2020). Green is the new white: How virtue motivates green product purchase. *Journal of Business Ethics*, *173*, 759–776.

Tabares, S. (2020). Insights from corporate social innovation: A research agenda. *Social Enterprise Journal*, *16*(3), 317–338.

Tangari, A. H., Folse, J. A. G., Burton, S., & Kees, J. (2010). The moderating influence of consumers' temporal orientation on the framing of societal needs and corporate responses in cause-related marketing campaigns. *Journal of Advertising*, *39*(2), 35–50.

Tezer, A., & Bodur, H. O. (2020). The greenconsumption effect: How using green products improves consumption experience. *Journal of Consumer Research*, *47*(1), 25–39.

Thomas, S., Kureshi, S., & Vatavwala, S. (2020). Cause-related marketing research (1988–2016): An academic review and classification. *Journal of Nonprofit & Public Sector Marketing*, *32*(5), 488–516.Trudel R. & Cotte, J (2009). Does it pay to be good? *MIT Sloan Management Review*, *50*, 61–68.

Van Marrewijk, M. (2003). Concepts and definitions of CSR and corporate sustainability: Between agency and communion. *Journal of Business Ethics, 44*(2), 95–105.

Varadarajan, P. R., & Menon, A. (1988). Cause-related marketing: A coalignment of marketing strategy and corporate philanthropy. *Journal of Marketing*, *52*(3), 58–74.

Varadarajan, R. (2017). Innovating for sustainability: A framework for sustainable innovations and a model of sustainable innovations orientation. *Journal of the Academy of Marketing Science*, *45*(1), 14–36.

Varadarajan, R., & Kaul, R. (2018). Doing well by doing good innovations: Alleviation of social problems in emerging markets through corporate SIs. *Journal of Business Research*, *86*(May), 225–233.

Vredenburg, J., Kapitan, S., Spry, A., & Kemper, J. A. (2020). Brands taking a stand: Authentic brand activism or woke washing? *Journal of Public Policy & Marketing*, *39*(4), 444–460.

Vrontis, D., Christofi, M., & Katsikeas, C. S. (2020). An assessment of the literature on cause-related marketing: implications for international competitiveness and marketing research. *International Marketing Review*, *37*(5), 977–1012.

Wagner, T., Lutz, R. J., & Weitz, B. A. (2009). Corporate hypocrisy: Overcoming the threat of inconsistent corporate social responsibility perceptions. *Journal of Marketing*, *73*, 77–91.

White, K., Habib, R., & Hardisty, D. J. (2019). How to SHIFT consumer behaviors to be more sustainable: A literature review and guiding framework. *Journal of Marketing*, *83*(3), 22–49.

Wright, C., & Nyberg, D. (2017). An inconvenient truth: How organizations translate climate change into business as usual. *Academy of Management Journal*, *60*(5), 1633–1661.

Yoon, Y., Gürhan-Canli, Z., & Schwartz, N. (2006). The effect of corporate social responsibility (CSR) activities on companies with bad reputations. *Journal of Consumer Psychology*, *16*(4), 377–390

4 Brands in Services

4.1 Introduction

Services dominate most economies today. The service sector accounts for a large share of the gross domestic product of industrialised countries and represents one of the largest employers. As consumers, we purchase services every day – be they retail banking, medical services, transportation, visiting travel agents, hairdressers, a supermarket or a restaurant. Given the growing managerial focus on managing the customer experience (CX), brands and services are invariably intertwined. Services span across all stages of the CX – from searching for purchase options, to the actual purchase decision, as well as post-purchase. Even businesses selling physical goods such as clothing have a noticeable service component in their offering given the need to both plan the delivery to the end consumer and offer post-purchase customer service.

Traditionally, services research focused on the provider–customer dyad. Increasingly, there is recognition that services are *experienced* in a complex service system consisting of configurations of people, technology and organisations. The issues of service provision, and how services are best managed and marketed, are therefore steadily gaining the attention of scholars as well as practitioners.

In scholarly research, studies on service quality, satisfaction, and CX have advanced understanding on brands in services. This chapter focuses on the foundations of service marketing theory. It takes into account the nature and characteristics of services, the marketing implications of intangibility, the importance of quality service in business practices and reviews the latest scholarly thinking in the area of CX management. The chapter also presents a number of avenues for future research in the domain.

DOI: 10.4324/9780429449598-4

4.2 The Origins of Service Branding

The field of services marketing originates from scholarly debate on the differentiation between goods marketing and services marketing. The work of scholars such as Leonard Berry, Christian Grönroos and Valarie Zeithaml has been seminal in this respect. Until the 1980s, despite the fast growth of services such as banking, insurance, accounting, the focus on the marketing of physical goods has been pervasive (Fisk et al., 1993). Gradually, the scholarly debate has advanced and delineated four distinctive characteristics of services, namely Intangibility, Heterogeneity, Inseparability, and Perishability, commonly referred to as the IHIP framework (see Edgett & Parkinson, 1993 and Zeithaml et al., 1985 for an overview). Intangibility concerns the intangible nature of services that cannot be seen or touched. This characteristic of services has been therefore associated with the difficulty encountered by consumers in evaluating the quality of a service and in differentiating between competing brands (Firth, 1993; Fitzgerald, 1988). As best exemplified by Zeithaml et al. (1985), services are 'performances' not objects that can be seen, tasted or touched (p. 33). Heterogeneity accounts for the variability of service performance mainly due to the human component inherent to service provision. Inseparability of production and consumption denotes the role of consumers as active contributors of the service experience, given their interaction with service providers (Dall'Olmo Riley & de Chernatony, 2000). Medical services or hairdressing, for instance, would not be delivered unless the customer is present. This makes consumers part of the service production and delivery processes, which tend to occur concurrently. Perishability can be explained by comparing physical goods which can stocked and shelved, and services which need to be consumed at the very same time that they are produced (Bateson, 1995), and at times do not even involve a transfer of ownership as in the case of access-based services (Schaefers et al., 2015).

Delineating the characteristics of services has been a pivotal step towards the advancement of knowledge on the role of branding in services. As elucidated by de Chernatony and Dall'Olmo Riley (1999), "whilst goods and services draw upon a common set of branding principles, there are differences in the emphasis given to specific tools" (p. 182). The dominant perspective has been that services marketing problems require services marketing solutions, and branding strategies originally developed from physical goods marketing are insufficient (Zeithaml et al., 1985). For instance, de Chernatony and Dall'Olmo Riley (1999) explain that branding strategies such as firm size and reputation are particularly meaningful signals of the quality of highly intangible services such as professional services. Likewise, corporate branding contributes to building a favourable disposition of the customer towards the service firm as well as reassurance when purchasing services, which are acquired long before the benefit of consumption can be realised (de Chernatony & Dall'Olmo Riley, 1999). As discussed further in Section 4.5, there is also growing evidence on the importance of brand equity and brand reputation in providing a buffer against negative service encounters. Furthermore, some scholars emphasise the importance of consumers' involvement in the production process so as to ensure that consumers' needs are better met, and service consumption is valued as a result (e.g., Roggeveen et al., 2012). The idea of consumers' involvement in the service production process is now well-established and commonly denoted as value co-creation. Internal branding is, by contrast, recognised as a meaningful strategy to enhance the homogeneity of service delivery. This view is consistent with the service profit chain framework asserting that positive employee attitude and behaviour can lead to increased quality and customer satisfaction, and in turn greater market share and sales growth (Heskett & Sasser, 2010).

A pioneering study on service branding by Berry (2000) suggests that branding is a 'cornerstone' of services marketing due to the difficulty of differentiating intangible offerings (p. 128). Given that the company is the primary brand not the physical offering, the actions and performance of corporates are invariably important in service settings. Berry (2000) also delineates advertising and external communications such as word of mouth as principal components of a service brand as these foster awareness of the brand and brand meaning, both conducive to building brand equity. The relevance of equity in service brands can be deduced by the sense of safety and reassurance that customers derive from strong brands, especially when acquiring intangible offerings that, at times, cannot be competently evaluated by consumers (e.g., hairdressing, medical services and car servicing).

Fundamental to Berry's theorising is the concept of brand meaning, which denotes "the customer's dominant perceptions of the brand" (p. 129). At the core of the idea of brand meaning is that branded and external communications contribute to building expectations of brand performance in consumers' mind, with their influence being most prominent among novel consumers without direct prior experience of the brand. Such expectations are later compared with the direct experience of the service, and consumers adjust their behaviour towards the brand accordingly. The mechanism is best exemplified by service quality models (Grönroos, 1984; Parasuraman et al., 1991) discussed further in Section 4.3. As highlighted by Berry (2000), "customers' experience-based beliefs are powerful" (p. 130). This means that consumers' direct experience of the brand accumulated over time tends to be disproportionately more influential than branded or external communications. As further discussed in Section 4.5, consumers' disappointment with the service brand experience is highly diagnostic towards influencing subsequent switching and negative word-of-mouth behaviour.

Overall, the work on the characteristics of services has been seminal in establishing services marketing as a sub-discipline of marketing, and in drawing a link between consumers and brands in services contexts. More recent theoretical advancements such as the service-dominant logic (Vargo & Lusch, 2016) have, however, challenged the view that services represent a field on their own simply due to the fact that services are increasingly at the core of what consumers need. Recent research has also questioned the IHIP framework on the grounds that technology has had a disruptive role (e.g., Bhanja & Saxena, 2022). In online banking, for instance, much of the heterogeneity of service delivery inherent to face-to-face interactions between employees at local branches and consumers has disappeared. Further research is warranted that empirically demonstrates the evolving nature of services, and accordingly, the relevance of branding strategies in a fast-changing technological landscape.

4.3 Service Brand Quality and Satisfaction

Understanding what consumers look for in the marketplace and what they evaluate in relation to service firms, thus also service brands, has been a question of notable interest among scholars (Grönroos, 1984; Parasuraman et al., 1988; 1991). In particular, substantial attention has been directed towards developing a model of service quality that could explicate how the quality of services is perceived by consumers. The assumption is that by understanding service quality, better service marketing strategies can be developed and executed. In this respect, the work of Grönroos (1984) is pivotal in laying out the conceptual foundations of service quality models, while Parasuraman and colleagues (1988, 1991) have substantially advanced empirical work. As elucidated by Grönroos (1984), consumer behaviour theory has informed some of the thinking around the need to consider expectations about performance to be able to explain post-consumption evaluations of services. In line with the work of Olshavsky and Miller (1972) and Anderson (1973), perceived quality has been conceptualised as the outcome of an evaluation process where consumers compare *expected* performance against *perceived* performance. Such a process applies to services where the brand's marketing communications set expectations in consumers' mind and such expectations are retrieved at the time that the service is experienced and evaluated. The literature further distinguishes between two dimensions of service quality – technical and functional. Technical quality concerns the instrumental performance of the service and related outcomes (Grönroos, 1984). For instance, a hotel room with all the necessary amenities for a guest to have an enjoyable stay represents the technical quality dimension. Equally important in services is functional quality, which denotes the production-related routines by which technical quality of the service is delivered (Grönroos, 1984). Taking the hotel example once again, the appearance and behaviour of staff at the reception desk or in the restaurant area are influential to shaping functional quality. In this sense, perceptions of the hotel service are holistic and encompassing evaluations of the hotel stay (i.e., technical quality) as well as the process by which that very same hotel stay has been delivered (i.e., functional quality).

As technology advances, much of the service provision is technology-mediated through a device (e.g., self-service machine), a website or even a robot. Extant research shows that, in the case of online service provision through an e-tail website, web aesthetics deliver both technical quality through a simple, easy-to-navigate design and functional quality through responsive service and meaningful web functionalities (e.g., Wang et al., 2010). Increasingly, in the online environment, hedonic quality in the form of the emotional outcome derived by consumers while contributing towards the service provision by using an interactive website or mobile application takes prominence. Hedonic quality is an important component of the value extracted by consumers through online service consumption, as evidenced by Bernardo et al. (2012). Based on a survey of consumers using online travel agency services, Bernardo et al. (2012) show that both functional quality (i.e., the functionality of the website in accomplishing the goals of consumers) and hedonic quality (i.e., perceived enjoyment of the website) have a positive and significant impact on perceived value.

In line with Olshavsky (1985) and the discussion above, quality is seen as 'perceived', rather than 'objective', as well as holistic, thus in the form of an overall attitude towards an offering. Exploratory data based on focus groups with consumers by Parasuraman et al. (1985) has confirmed that, regardless of the type of service, consumers rely on very similar criteria when asked to evaluate service quality. Scholarly thinking has also unambiguously found support for the notion that service quality, as perceived by consumers, results from a comparison of what they expect from the service firm and their perceptions of the service delivered (Grönroos, 1982; 1984; Parasuraman et al., 1985). Finally, perceived quality is multifaceted, which means that multiple criteria are employed by consumers to deduce quality (Parasuraman et al., 1985). The criteria somehow reflect the dimensions of technical quality (e.g., reliability, competence) and functional quality (e.g., communication, responsiveness) discussed by Grönroos (1984).

Grounded on the above precepts, Parasuraman et al. (1988; 1991) have developed the SERVQUAL instrument to measuring service quality across a variety of settings. SERVQUAL is founded on the expectancy disconfirmation paradigm of satisfaction (Oliver, 1980; Oliver & DeSarbo, 1988). According to this paradigm, consumers form expectations of product performance prior to purchase. Actual performance evaluations obtained through usage are compared to expectation levels using a better-than, worse-than heuristic. Such a comparison is labelled as *negative disconfirmation of expectations* if actual performance is worse than expected, and *positive disconfirmation of expectations* if the service performance is better than expected, or simple confirmation if the service performance is as expected. Accordingly, the SERVQUAL instrument captures the GAP between what consumers *expect* from service brands and what they actually *experience* in relation to five dimensions of quality, namely reliability, assurance, tangibles, empathy, responsiveness.

Given the fast growth of online services, scholars have directed attention towards developing instruments that could capture quality in such contexts. Examples of such instruments include E-S-QUAL measuring electronic service quality (Parasuraman et al., 2005), e-SELFQUAL tapping into online self-service quality (Ding et al., 2011), service quality in e-retailing (Collier & Bienstock, 2006) and eTransQual capturing transactional quality with online shopping (Bauer et al., 2006). Further research in the domain is required, especially in the light of the transformation of services through the influence of Artificial Intelligence (AI). The traditional drivers of service quality need to be reinvestigated to establish their applicability to service-based AI contexts where humans are partially or completely replaced by AI and/or robots as in the case of chatbots (see Bock et al., 2020, for a review of future research opportunities).

Notwithstanding its popularity, SERVQUAL has not been short of criticisms. Among other aspects, the most prominent criticism concerns the variability of individuals' expectations and the appropriateness of the gaps model. As best exemplified by Buttle (1996), "the term expectation is polysemic; consumers use standards other than expectations to evaluate service quality" (p. 11). This implies that capturing expectations might provide an erroneous evaluation of quality. Crucially, the similarity between the satisfaction model from Oliver (1980) and the measurement of service quality has casted doubts on the instrument and the extent to which SERVQUAL and customer satisfaction do in fact tap into very similar constructs (Iacobucci et al., 1994). Overall, there is scholarly consensus that perceived quality of service attributes is associated with customer satisfaction, which in turn impacts loyalty (e.g., Chiou & Droge, 2006). Furthermore, the work of Babakus and Boller (1992) suggests that, in capturing the gap score, the dominant contributors are the perceptions not the expectations of quality given a generalised response tendency to rate expectations high. Accordingly, Cronin and Taylor (1992) have proposed a performance-based measure of service quality, labelled as SERVPERF, and found that the latter instrument explains more variance of service quality than SERVQUAL. Undoubtedly, the SERVQUAL instrument remains a valuable tool to marketing academia and practice. Applications of the instrument are far wide ranging across a variety of industrial, commercial and not-for-profit settings (see Ladhari, 2009 for a review of 20 years of SERVQUAL research). The topic of service quality has, over the years, evolved further. More recent discussion in the service community concerns the concept of service experience, as discussed in Section 4.4.

4.4 Service Brand Experience – Touchpoints, Customer Journey

Relationships have long been recognised as important in services. Dall'Olmo Riley and de Chernatony (2000) argue that the brand acts as a 'relationship builder' or 'relationship fulcrum' in services. The service brand is seen to provide the link between internal factors, such as those concerned with employees, and external encounters with consumers, as both consumers' and employees' relationships with a brand are important in services marketing. The 1990s witnessed emerging attention on the idea of developing relationships with customers. Initially conceived in B2B settings (e.g., Dwyer et al., 1987; Geyskens et al., 1998) and later adopted in consumer markets (Berry, 1995; Sheth & Parvatiyar, 1995), relationship marketing literature has brought forth a focus on the concepts of trust, commitment and relationship quality (Lemon & Verhoef, 2016). Additionally, attention has been directed towards the emotional aspects of customer relationships (Verhoef & Lemon, 2015) with constructs such as passion and intimacy being measured (Bügel et al., 2011). Relationship marketing has notably augmented the focus on CX.

The concept of CX has been discussed in various bodies of literature for over 80 years and recently it has been the major focus of service research and practice. CX is grounded on the idea, already advanced in the fields of economics and psychology, that pure economic rationality does not fully explain consumer behaviour. In fact, emotional aspects of customer relationships with brands are highly important (Verhoef & Lemon, 2015). With the advent of Total Quality Management (TQM), the focus on CX became prominent. TQM, a concept popularised in Japan, was an American response to the Japanese multinationals using quality to gain markets. TQM applied cross-functional business process management to manufacturing and distribution successfully, reducing costs, improving quality and increasing availability. Sustained by success in manufacturing, the idea transferred to management and service branding particularly. In a famous Harvard article, Reichheld and Sasser (1990) augured that 'Quality Comes to Service'.

The above perspective builds on literature suggesting that best practices in quality mass production could be transferred to service businesses (Levitt, 1976; Shostack, 1984). The quality 'revolution' has been combined with growing scholarly interest in services marketing to understand the impact of service quality upon brand, relationships and performance (Dagger et al., 2007; Falk et al., 2010; Richard & Allaway, 1993). The SERVQUAL instrument discussed in Section 4.3 has been influential in this scholarly debate. Whilst recognising the importance of quality, scholars have gradually reached a consensus that quality only represents one aspect of a broader concept called CX (Verhoef & Lemon, 2015). Experience has been defined as "a multidimensional construct focusing on a customer's cognitive, emotional, behavioral, sensorial, and social responses to a firm's offerings during the customer's entire purchase journey" (Lemon & Verhoef, 2016, p. 71). Unsurprisingly, the measures of quality earlier developed by Parasuraman and colleagues have been replaced by newly developed measures of CX (e.g., Klaus & Maklan, 2012).

As evidenced by the definition above, CX is based on a journey with a brand where the consumer goes through the purchase cycle and engages with a brand and its representatives on multiple occasions (Lemon & Verhoef, 2016). The journey typically entails the prepurchase, purchase and post-purchase stages (Neslin et al., 2006; Pucinelli et al., 2009). During the journey, customers interact with the brand on a variety of touchpoints (see De Keyser et al., 2020 for details on the nomenclature). Lemon and Verhoef (2016) refer to brand-owned, partner-owned, customer-owned, and social/external/independent touchpoints, depending on whether the brand, its partners, other consumers or all of these stakeholders interact with consumers and contribute towards influencing the CX. The nature of the product/service or the consumer's own journey makes one or the other touchpoints more or less relevant at certain purchase stages. For instance, the atmospherics created by the brand are particularly important touchpoints at the purchase stage in retail experiences.

In the light of the growing adoption of the online channel, much scholarly research has examined online customer experiences. In the context of e-retailing, Rose et al. (2012) discuss the drivers of cognitive and affective experiential state of consumers, both representing key components of the online CX on Internet shopping websites. Through a series of experimental studies, Bleier et al. (2019) have advanced this field by establishing the link between four dimensions of the online CX (informativeness, entertainment, social presence and sensory appeal) and purchase. Further, in studying CX in the online space, the concept of *flow* has received notable attention. First conceptualised by Hoffman and Novak (1996), flow denotes a cognitive state experienced during navigation on the web which is linked to perceived control, arousal, attention span and enabled interactivity. The construct has also received some empirical verification (e.g., Novak et al., 2000). While the offline versus online dichotomy proves useful from an empirical standpoint, in practice consumers tend to be channel agnostic. Touchpoints via the online channel (e.g., consumers visiting an e-tail site to search for the desired product) can be as relevant in offline experiences (e.g., consumers visit the physical retail store to finalise the purchase). Further research is needed that addresses the interplay of touchpoints regardless of the channel involved.

In essence, the notion of CX has broadened earlier thinking on consumers and service brands (see Becker & Jaakkola, 2020 for a recent review of the field). In particular, in this literature domain, emotional responses to brand stimuli are recognised as being equally important to consumers' cognitive evaluations such as satisfaction. Quality is an antecedent of CX (e.g., Mittal et al., 1999) while trust and commitment are consequences of experiences (e.g., Lemon & Verhoef, 2016). CX design is an aspect that has garnered attention, with the service blueprinting approach being highly influential in marketing academia and practice (see detailed discussion on the approach in Bitner et al., 2008 and Patricio et al., 2011). Within this body of work, there has also been interest in understanding consumer responses to touchpoints that fail to deliver upon the brand's promise causing dissatisfaction, also commonly referred to as service failures (Berry et al., 2002). The research evidence in service failure and recovery literature is discussed in Section 4.5.

Several aspects of CX management, however, merit further scholarly attention. Extant research adopts a micro approach focusing on specific brands or industries. In practice, consumers face several experiences concurrently, and the experience in one setting might spill over to other domains, contexts, situations and industries (Lemon & Verhoef, 2016). Future research could address this aspect more explicitly. Relatedly, as brands find new channels to interact with consumers, experience design and management increase in complexity. Novel data are required to capture social touchpoints, such as consumer interactions with the brand via influencers. Scholars are also calling for the development of scales for measuring CX across the entire customer journey (Lemon & Verhoef, 2016) and research that explains how social touchpoints, which are not controlled by brands, affect CX of brand-owned touchpoints (De Keyser et al., 2020).

4.5 Service Brand Failure and Recovery Management

Research on service failure and recovery has been abundant over the past 20 years or so. Scholars agree that failures cannot be fully prevented by service brands given the heterogeneity of delivery and customer reactions. Service failures represent "any service-related mishaps or problems (real and/or perceived) that occur during a consumer's experience with the firm" (Maxham, 2001, p. 11). In response to a service failure, consumers tend to experience negative disconfirmation of expectations, thus dissatisfaction (Oliver & DeSarbo, 1988). Dissatisfaction is often combined with negative emotions, such as disappointment and regret (Zeelenberg & Pieters, 2004), anger, frustration and helplessness (e.g., Antonetti et al., 2020; Bougie et al., 2003; Gelbrich, 2010; Kalamas et al., 2008). The attribution of blame to the brand is a frequent mechanism to establish responsibility for the failure event and appraise emotions and behaviour (Hess et al., 2003). Overall, service failures are important moments-of-truth as such events are likely to affect consumers' overall experience with the brand and their subsequent complaining and switching behaviour.

Remarkably, evidence in the domain suggests that even following a service failure that causes anger and complaining, consumers are unlikely to exit the relationship with the brand (Voorhees et al., 2006). Such an effect has been explained through the lens of hierarchical theories of emotions suggesting that anger is one of the fundamental 'emotion prototypes' (Shaver et al., 1987) or 'emotional modes' (Johnson-Laird & Oatley, 1989), which can manifest itself in several specific forms. In this sense, there is no one single form of anger. In the work of Antonetti et al. (2020), qualitative and experimental data concerning consumers' negative experiences with service brands show that anger can be of two types – supportive and vindictive. Supportive anger is low arousal, mild, includes feelings of annoyance and frustration, and is motivated by a desire for reconciliation and to find a resolution to the problem. By contrast, vindictive anger is high arousal, includes feelings of rage and outrage, and is motivated by a desire for retaliation and to seek revenge against the brand. Such advancements in understanding the psychology of emotional responses in service failures have enriched the domain and have found applications in management practice.

Regardless of whether consumers respond to service failures with retaliation or reconciliation, service brands are expected to respond to such events. Firms recur to service recovery, namely actions aimed at rectifying the problem and restore the consumer–brand relationship (Singh & Crisafulli, 2015). Examples of service recovery include compensation, discounts, upgraded or free services, and/or apology. Effective service recovery can enhance perceptions of service quality, firm competence, customer satisfaction and, ultimately, loyalty (Boshoff, 1997). On certain occasions, though very rare, customer satisfaction with recovery is even higher than satisfaction prior to the failure, resulting in a peculiar effect termed the service recovery paradox (SRP). Magnini et al. (2007) show that the SRP is more likely to occur when the service failure causes a minor inconvenience (low severity), is out of the control of the service brand (low controllability) and is unlikely to reoccur (low stability). Overall, the evidence on the occurrence of SRP is mixed. The work by Ok et al. (2007) suggests that recovery efforts need to be exceptional rather than just good for SRP to occur. When recovery is just good, the negative effect of service failures cannot be mitigated and initial overall satisfaction is carried over. When recovery is poor or fails as in the event of double deviations, whereby both the service provision and recovery fail, SRP is also unlikely to occur.

In an attempt to explain the psychological mechanism influencing consumer responses to brands' recovery efforts, scholars have relied upon social exchange theory (i.e., equity theory, justice theory; e.g., Smith et al., 1999), resource exchange theory (e.g., Roschk & Gelbrich, 2014) or social resource theory (e.g., Roschk & Gelbrich, 2017). The prevailing view is that consumers incur a resource loss as a result of the service failure (e.g., a loss of money) and such a loss should be offset with similar resources (i.e., monetary compensation, e.g., Roschk &

Gelbrich, 2014). There is ample empirical evidence that consumers look for fair (or just) service recovery. Justice can be achieved by means of, delivering a fair compensation, whether tangible (e.g., refund) or psychological (e.g., apology), providing a timely response and by showing empathy towards the customer, or else, by a combination of all these aspects (Singh & Crisafulli, 2015). The meta-analysis by Gelbrich and Roschk (2011) confirms the mediating role of perceived justice dimensions in explaining the impact of organisational responses to service failures and customer behavioural responses in the form of loyalty and positive word of mouth.

Concurrently, there is growing evidence on the pivotal role of existing brand associations in acting as a 'buffer' against service failures including for instance brand equity (Brady et al., 2008). Likewise, the brand's CSR efforts are found to provide a buffer against the negative impact of product failures (Chernev & Blair, 2015) and cases of corporate irresponsibility, especially when the latter concern other domains than the ones where the brand makes explicit commitments (Lenz et al., 2017), and when service failures signal the brand's lack of skills and expertise (Antonetti et al., 2021). Consumers are willing to give brands known for CSR the benefit of the doubt, provided that information about irresponsible behaviour does not directly contradict pre-existing perceptions (Vanhamme & Grobben, 2009). CSR is found to enhance perceived warmth of the brand if the service failure denotes lack of competence, not if the brand's integrity is at stake, and enhanced warmth does in turn lowers revenge (Antonetti et al., 2021).

All in all, the field of service failure and recovery is at an advanced stage (see Grégoire & Mattila, 2021 for a review). A hitherto overlooked area concerns Artificial Intelligence (AI)-enabled services wherein failures occur. Brands attempting recovery following AI-enabled services face challenges associated with the lack of interaction between consumers and employees. While on the one hand, consumers might be more forgiving of brands in the presence of AI, on the other hand, AI could trigger frustration and other negative emotions that could escalate easily. Another research avenue could focus on the role of co-creation in service recovery. Through co-created service recovery, consumers are given the ability to "shape or personalize the content of the service recovery through joint collaboration with the service provider" (Roggeveen et al., 2012, p. 772). The relevance of co-creation in service recovery finds theoretical grounding in value co-creation literature, which sees consumers as active (not passive) creators of value integrating resources with the company (Vargo & Lusch, 2016). Evidence suggests that consumers participation in service recovery is perceived as a signal of fair interpersonal treatment and just redress (Van Vaerenberg et al., 2018), which leads to enhanced brand identification (Antonetti & Crisafulli, 2022). Co-creation might also give consumers a sense of agency over the company and the service experience. Such a sense of agency, however, could have contradictory effects. Agency could prompt consumers to take action themselves in the event of service failures in such a way that benefits brands, or else, agency could create a strong sense of entitlement that backfires service brands especially so if recurrent service failures occur. The above area merits further research. Further, substantial amount of research on service failure and recovery focuses on the customer–brand dyad (Grégoire & Mattila, 2021). Future research could consider new contexts beyond this dyad. Lastly, extant evidence is based on an analysis of discrete organisational actions and their impact on consumer perceptions and behaviour. In practice, there is growing awareness of the dynamic nature of the recovery experience, with service failure and recovery being one component of a much larger and complex overall experience with the brand. Scholars have thus coined the term of service recovery journey (Van Vaerenberg et al., 2019) and called for research that explores the interaction of variables at pre-recovery, recovery and post-recovery phases of the journey.

4.6 New Developments in Service Branding Research

A growing field of research addresses issues concerning how services delivered by brands affect aspects of life, thus individual well-being. This stream of work is commonly referred to as transformative service research (TSR). First conceptualised by Anderson (2010), TSR research investigates the relationship between service provision and individual and/or collective well-being. In particular, it concerns studies focusing on creating 'uplifting changes' to the lives of individuals, whether consumers, employees, communities and society at large (Anderson et al., 2013). The most notable contributions to this stream of work have been published in a 2015 special issue by the *Journal of Service Research*, edited by Anderson and Ostrom. Extant studies address three key themes: (1) the well-being implications of negative service and value destruction, (2) how value is created collectively and the implications for well-being, and (3) consumers' roles and activities in cocreating value with brands and the effect on well-being. With respect to the first theme, the work of Spanjol et al. (2015) is notable in that it illustrates how, in negative service contexts wherein chronically ill patients need to adhere to medication, coproduction of value occurs inside the consumer sphere more than with the service brand. With regards to the second theme, the work of Yao et al. (2015) is insightful in that it shows how social, peer-to-peer support of individuals with chronic diseases improves quality of life. Such a finding demonstrates that service brands' efforts in supporting consumers can expand beyond the boundaries of the organisation and involve communities of consumers. Lastly, in relation to the third theme, the work of Martin and Hill (2015) offers evidence on the role of service brands in supporting populations around the world that live at the base of the pyramid (BoP). Their data spanning across 38 countries and 50,000 consumers shows that saving is most effective at enhancing the well-being of societies with high levels of poverty. The work provides implications for financial services development at the BoP.

Another contemporary and fascinating stream of work concerns the role of technology in service provision. Prior studies have investigated a variety of themes, including how self-service technologies (SSTs) impact consumer evaluations (e.g., Zhu et al. 2007), the effect of automated social presence (e.g., van Doorn et al., 2017) and augmented reality technologies (e.g., Hilken et al., 2017) on CX, consumers' barriers and facilitators to the adoption of smart interactive services such as remote diagnosis and remote repair services (Wünderlich et al., 2013). Long-standing issues concerning service failure and recovery management have also been revisited in the context of technology-enhanced service provision (e.g., Zhu et al., 2013). Most recently, scholarly attention has shifted towards AI and service robots in particular (e.g., Huang & Rust, 2018, 2021; Wirtz et al., 2018, 2021). Service robots are considered autonomous agents, whether physically embodied or virtual (e.g., voice- or text-based chatbots), with the core purpose of performing physical and nonphysical tasks to ensure the provision of services to consumers (Joerling et al., 2019). There is a notable amount of research examining the impact of anthropomorphism, wherein robots have a human shape, show human characteristics, or imitate human behaviour, on consumer use of a robot. Extant evidence presents conflicting findings, with studies showing positive, neutral or even negative effects on consumers (Goudey & Bonnin, 2016; Stroessner & Benitez, 2019). The meta-analysis by Blut et al. (2021) partly reconciles existing evidence showing that anthropomorphism exerts a positive effect on consumers' intentions to re-use the robot. In particular, the robot characteristics of animacy, intelligence, likability, safety and social presence as well as perceived usefulness and ease of use of robots explain how anthropomorphism translates into future use intentions.

Notwithstanding the popularity of AI-enabled services, there are scholars cautioning against using AI as a silver bullet. In a conceptual piece, Huang and Rust (2021) advocate for a tailored use of AI that accounts for the nature of the service task, the type of service offering, the service strategy, and the service process. The same authors go further to explain that while mechanical service tasks (e.g., shipping, delivery, payment) can be performed mostly by mechanical AI, thinking service tasks (e.g., identify new market, personalise service) require human intelligence combined with AI, yet feeling service tasks (e.g., engage and interact with customers, personalise customer service) warrant mostly human intelligence. When it comes to AI in services, future research could shed light on the degree of autonomy that consumers wish to retain when dealing with autonomous services. Further, research has started to investigate how service robots' perceptions influence brand trust and brand experience (Blut et al., 2018; Chan & Tung, 2019). More work is needed to address how perceptions of a service robot may spill over to the brand employing the robot. Individual characteristics of consumers as well as contextual factors might play an important role in shaping the adoption of service robots and subsequent perceptions. Preliminary evidence, for instance, shows that consumers' technological optimism increases, while perceived insecurity decreases intentions to use robo-advisors (Flavián et al., 2022). Outcomes of transformative research such as physical and mental well-being could also be relevant and worth investigating (Blut et al., 2021). Increasingly, service robots (e.g., chatbots) are being employed by brands as substitutes of human service providers in customer service and complaint management roles. A fruitful area for research concerns whether and how robots can diminish negative attributions about the brand when the experience fails to be satisfactory. Preliminary evidence on attributions of responsibility when consumers deal with service robots indicates that while consumers are more likely to attribute responsibility for a negative outcome to themselves than to the robot or the brand, such attributions elicit negative emotions which tend to cloud the service experience (Joerling et al., 2019). Furthermore, there is evidence that, unlike nonhumanoid service robots, humanoid ones are perceived to be warmer, yet create greater dissatisfaction when service failures demonstrate a lack of warmth towards the customer (Choi et al., 2021).

In the area of TSR, an avenue for further research concerns the impact of services and service systems on poor consumers' well-being, and more generally, populations at the Base of the Pyramid (Anderson & Ostrom, 2015). Further, research in services has often been grounded on the assumption that service provision and associated value co-creation processes are accepted by consumers at face value. In practice, there is evidence that service provision can cause stress to service employees acting as representatives of the brand (Chan et al., 2010). In a similar way, consumers might experience stress from engaging in value co-creation processes. The case of medical services is exemplary in this respect, wherein consumers need to balance efforts to adhere to medical advice while also preserving their need for autonomy. The above illustrates that both TSR and AI in services are areas of work gaining footing, yet warranting additional empirical research.

References

Anderson, L. (2010). Improving well-being through transformative service. In Ostrom, A. L., Bitner, M. J., Brown, S. W., Burkhard, K. A., Goul, M., Smith-Daniels, V., Demirkan, H., & Rabinovich, E. (eds), Moving forward and making a difference: Research priorities for the science of service, by *Journal of Service Research*, *13*(1), 4–36.

Anderson, L., & Ostrom, A. L. (2015). Transformative service research: Advancing our knowledge about service and well-being. *Journal of Service Research*, *18*(3), 243–249.

Anderson, L., Ostrom, A. L., Corus, C., Fisk, R. P., Gallan, A. S., Giraldo, M., Mende, M., Mulder, M., Rayburn, S. W., Rosenbaum, M. S., Shirahada, K., & Williams, J. D. (2013). Transformative service research: An agenda for the future. *Journal of Business Research*, *66*(8), 1203–1210.

Anderson, R. E. (1973). Consumer dissatisfaction: The effect of discontinued expectancy on perceived product performance. *Journal of Marketing Research*, *10*(1), 38–44.

Antonetti, P. & Crisafulli, B. (2022). Revisiting power messaging in service failures: Pitfalls and proposed solutions. *Psychology & Marketing*, ISSN 0742-6046.

Antonetti, P., Crisafulli, B., & Katsikeas, C. (2020). Does it really hurt? Making sense of varieties of anger. *Psychology & Marketing*, *37*(11), 1465–1483.

Antonetti, P., Crisafulli, B., & Maklan, S. (2021). When doing good will not save us: Revisiting the buffering effect of CSR following service failures. *Psychology & Marketing*, *38*(9), 1608–1627.

Babakus, E., & Boller, G. W. (1992). An empirical assessment of the SERVQUAL scale. *Journal of Business Research*, *24*, 253–268.

Bateson, J. E. G. (1995). *Managing Services Marketing*. London: The Dryden Press.

Bauer, H. H., Falk, T., & Hammerschmidt, M. (2006). eTransQual: A transaction process-based approach for capturing service quality in online shopping. *Journal of Business Research*, *59*(7), 866–875.

Becker, L., & Jaakkola, E. (2020). Customer experience: Fundamental premises and implications for research. *Journal of the Academy of Marketing Science*, *48*, 630–648.

Bernardo, M., Marimon, F., & del Mar Alonso-Almeida, M. (2012). Functional quality and hedonic quality: A study of the dimensions of e-service quality in online travel agencies. *Information & Management*, *49*, 342–347.

Berry, L. L. (1995). Relationship marketing of services—Growing interest, emerging perspectives. *Journal of the Academy of Marketing Science, 23*(4), 236–245.

Berry, L. L. (2000). Cultivating service brand equity. *Journal of the Academy of Marketing Science, 28*(1), 128–137.

Berry, L. L., Seiders, K., & Grewal, D. (2002). Understanding service convenience. *Journal of Marketing, 66* (July), 1–17.

Bhanja, N., & Saxena, G. (2022). Revisiting the past to understand the current debates on service-dominant logic. *Services Marketing Quarterly, 43*(2), 240–255.

Bitner, M. J., Ostrom, A. L., & Morgan, F. N. (2008). Service blueprinting: A practical technique for service innovation. *California Management Review, 50*(3), 66–94.

Bleier, A., Harmeling, C. M., & Palmatier, R. W. (2019). Creating effective online customer experiences. *Journal of Marketing, 83*(2), 98–119.

Blut, M., Teller, C., & Floh, A. (2018). Testing retail marketing-mix effects on patronage: A meta-analysis. *Journal of Retailing, 94*(2), 113–135.

Blut, M., Wang, C., Wünderlich, N. V., & Brock, C. (2021). Understanding anthropomorphism in service provision: A meta-analysis of physical robots, chatbots, and other AI. *Journal of the Academy of Marketing Science, 49*(4), 632–658.

Bock, D. E., Wolter, J. S., & Ferrell, O. C. (2020). Artificial intelligence: Disrupting what we know about services. *Journal of Services Marketing, 34*(3), 317–334.

Boshoff, C. (1997). An experimental study of service recovery options. *International Journal of Service Industry Management, 8*(2), 110–130.

Bougie, R., Pieters, R., & Zeelenberg, M. (2003). Angry customers don't come back, they get back: The experience and behavioral implications of anger and dissatisfaction in services. *Journal of the Academy of Marketing Science, 31*(4), 377–393.

Brady, M. K., Cronin Jr., J. L., Fox, G. L., & Roehm, M. L. (2008). Strategies to offset performance failures: The role of brand equity. *Journal of Retailing, 84*(2), 151–164.

Bügel, M. S., Verhoef, P. C. & Buunk, A. P. (2011). Customer intimacy and commitment to relationships with firms in five different sectors: Preliminary evidence. *Journal of Retailing and Consumer Services, 18*(4), 247–258.

Buttle, F. (1996). SERVQUAL: Review, critique, research agenda. *European Journal of Marketing, 30*(1), 8–32.

Chan, A. P. H., & Tung, V. W. S. (2019). Examining the effects of robotic service on brand experience: The moderating role of hotel segment. *Journal of Travel & Tourism Marketing, 36*(4), 458–468.

Chan, K. W., Yim, C. K., & Lam, S. S. K. (2010). Is customer participation in value creation a double-edged sword? Evidence from professional financial services across cultures. *Journal of Marketing, 74*(May), 48–64.

Chernev, A., & Blair, S. (2015). Doing well by doing good: The benevolent halo of corporate social responsibility. *Journal of Consumer Research, 41*(6), 1412–1425.

Chiou, J.-S., & Droge, C. (2006). Service quality, trust, specific asset investment, and expertise: Direct and indirect effects in a satisfaction-loyalty framework. *Journal of the Academy of Marketing Science, 34*(4), 613–627.

Choi, S., Mattila, A. S., & Bolton, L. E. (2021). To Err is Human(-oid): How do consumers react to robot service failure and recovery? *Journal of Service Research, 24*(3), 354–371.

Collier, J. E., & Bienstock, C. C. (2006). Measuring service quality in e-retailing. Journal of Service Research, *8*(3), 260–275.

Cronin, J. J. Jr and Taylor, S. A. (1992). Measuring service quality: A reexamination and extension. *Journal of Marketing, 56*(July), 55–68.

Dagger, T. S., Sweeney, J. C., & Johnson, L. W. (2007). A hierarchical model of health service quality: Scale development and investigation of an integrated model. *Journal of Service Research, 10*(2), 123–142.

Dall'Olmo Riley, F., & de Chernatony, L. (2000). The service brand as a relationship builder. *British Journal of Management, 11*, 137–150.

de Chernatony, L., & Dall'Olmo Riley, F. (1999). Experts' views about defining services brands and the principles of services branding. *Journal of Business Research, 46*(2), 181–192.

De Keyser, A., Verleye, K., Lemon, K. N., Keiningham, T. L., & Klaus, P. (2020). Moving the customer experience field forward: Introducing the touchpoints, context, qualities (TCQ) nomenclature. *Journal of Service Research, 23*(4), 433–455.

Ding, X. D., Hu, P. J.-H., & Liu Sheng, O. R. (2011). e-SELFQUAL: A scale for measuring online self-service quality. *Journal of Business Research, 64*(5), 508–515.

Dwyer, F. R., Schurr, P. H., & Oh, S. (1987). Developing buyer-seller relationships. *Journal of Marketing, 51*(2), 11–27.

Edgett, S., & Parkinson, S. (1993). Marketing for service industries - A review. *The Service Industries Journal, 13*(3), 19–39.

Falk, T., Hammerschmidt, M., & Schepers, J. J. L. (2010). The service quality-satisfaction link revisited: Exploring asymmetries and dynamics. *Journal of the Academy of Marketing Science, 38*, 288–302.

Firth, M. (1993). Price setting and the value of a strong brand name. *International Journal of Research in Marketing, 10*(December), 381–386.

Fisk, R. P., Brown, S. W., & Bitner, M. J. (1993). Tracking the evolution of services marketing literature. *Journal of Retailing, 69*(1), 61–103.

Fitzgerald, T. J. (1988). Understanding the differences and similarities between services and products to exploit your competitive advantage. *Journal of Services Marketing, 2*(Winter), 25–30.

Flavián, C., Pérez-Rueda, A., Belanche, D., & Casaló, L. V. (2022). Intention to use analytical artificial intelligence (AI) in services – the effect of technology readiness and awareness. *Journal of Service Management, 33*(2), 293–320.

Gelbrich, K. (2010). Anger, frustration, and helplessness after service failure: Coping strategies and effective informational support. *Journal of the Academy of Marketing Science, 38*(5), 567–585.

Gelbrich, K., & Roschk, H. (2011). A meta-analysis of organizational complaint handling and customer responses. *Journal of Service Research, 14*(1), 24–43.

Geyskens, I., Steenkamp, J.-B. E. M., & Kumar, N. (1998). Generalizations about trust in marketing channel relationships using meta-analysis. *International Journal of Research in Marketing, 15*(3), 223–248.

Goudey, A., & Bonnin, G. (2016). Must smart objects look human? Recherche et Applications en *Marketing, 31*(2), 2–20.

Grégoire, Y., & Mattila, A. S. (2021). Service failure and recovery at the crossroads: Recommendations to revitalize the field and its influence. *Journal of Service Research, 24*(3), 323–328.

Grönroos, C. (1982). *Strategic Management and Marketing in the Service Sector.* Helsinki: Swedish School of Economics and Business Administration.

Grönroos, C. (1984). A service quality model and its marketing implications. European *Journal of Marketing, 18*, 36–44.

Heskett, J. L., Sasser, W. E. (2010). The Service Profit Chain. In *Handbook of Service Science. Service Science: Research and Innovations in the Service Economy*, Maglio, P., Kieliszewski, C., Spohrer, J. (Eds). Boston, MA: Springer.

Hess Jr., R. L., Ganesan, S., & Klein, N. M. (2003). Service failure and recovery: The impact of relationship factors on customer satisfaction. *Journal of the Academy of Marketing Science, 31*(2), 127–145.

Hilken, T., de Ruyter, K., Chylinski, M., Mahr, D., & Keeling, D. I. (2017). Augmenting the eye of the beholder: Exploring the strategic potential of augmented reality to enhance online service experiences. *Journal of the Academy of Marketing Science, 45*, 884–905.

Hoffman, D. L., & Novak, T. P. (1996). Marketing in hypermedia computer-mediated environments: Conceptual foundations. *Journal of Marketing, 60*(3), 50–68.

Huang, M. H., & Rust, R. T. (2018). Artificial intelligence in service. *Journal of Service Research, 21*(2), 155–172.

Huang, M. H., & Rust, R. T. (2021). Engaged to a robot? The role of AI in service. *Journal of Service Research, 24*(1), 30–41.

Iacobucci, D., Grayson, K. A. & Omstrom, A. L. (1994). The calculus of service quality and customer satisfaction: Theoretical and empirical differentiation and integration. In *Advances in Services Marketing and Management*, Swartz, T.A., Bowen, D.E. and Brown, S.W. (Eds), Greenwich, CT: JAI Press (Vol. 3; pp. 1–68).

Joerling, M., Böhm, R., & Paluch, S. (2019). Service robots: Drivers of perceived responsibility for service outcomes. *Journal of Service Research, 22*(4), 404–420.

Johnson-Laird, P. N. & Oatley, K. (1989). The language of emotions: An analysis of a semantic field. *Cognition and Emotion, 3*(2), 81–123.

Kalamas, M., Laroche, M., & Makdessian, L. (2008). Reaching the boiling point: Consumers' negative affective reactions to firm-attributed service failures. *Journal of Business Research, 61*(8), 813–824.

Klaus, P. & Maklan, S. (2012). EXQ: A multiple-item scale for assessing service experience. *Journal of Service Management, 23*(1), 5–33.

Ladhari, R. (2009). A review of twenty years of SERVQUAL research. *International Journal of Quality and Service Sciences, 1*(2), 172–198.

Lemon, K. N., & Verhoef, P. C. (2016). Understanding customer experience throughout the customer journey. *Journal of Marketing, 80*(6), 69–96.

Lenz, I., Wetzel, H. A., & Hammerschmidt, M. (2017). Can doing good lead to doing poorly? Firm value implications of CSR in the face of CSI. *Journal of the Academy of Marketing Science, 45*(5), 677–697.

Levitt, T. (1976). The industrialization of service. *Harvard Business Review, 54*(September–October), 63–74.

Magnini, V. P., Ford, J. B., Markowski, E. P., & Honeycutt Jr., E. D. (2007). The service recovery paradox: Justifiable theory or smoldering myth? *Journal of Services Marketing, 21*(3), 213–225.

Martin, K. D., & Hill, R. P. (2015). Saving and well-being at the base of the pyramid: Implications for transformative financial services delivery. *Journal of Service Research, 18*(3), 405–421.

Maxham III, J. G. (2001). Service recovery's influence on consumer satisfaction, positive word-of- mouth and purchase intentions. *Journal of Business Research, 54*(1), 11–24.

Mittal, V., Kumar, P., & Tsiros, M. (1999). Attribute-level performance, satisfaction, and behavioral intentions over time: A consumption-system approach. *Journal of Marketing, 63*(April), 88–101.

Neslin, S. A., Grewal, D., Leghorn, R., Shankar, V., Teerling, M. L., Thomas, J. S. et al. (2006). Challenges and opportunities in multichannel customer management. *Journal of Service Research, 9*(2), 95–112.

Novak, T. P., Hoffman, D. L., & Yung, Y.-F. (2000). Measuring the customer experience in online environments: A structural modeling approach. *Marketing Science, 19*(1), 1–104.

Ok, C., Back, K. J., & Shanklin, C. W. (2007). Mixed findings on the service recovery paradox. *The Service Industries Journal, 27*(6), 671–686.

Oliver, R. L. (1980). A cognitive model of the antecedents and consequences of satisfaction decisions. *Journal of Marketing Research, 17*(November), 460–469.

Oliver, R. L., & DeSarbo, W. S. (1988). Response determinants in satisfaction judgments. *Journal of Consumer Research, 14*(4), 495–507.

Olshavsky, R. W. (1985). Toward a more comprehensive theory of choice. In *ACR North American Advances*, Hirschman, Elizabeth C. and Holbrook, Moris B. Provo, UT: Association for Consumer Research (Vol. 12; pp. 465–470).

Olshavsky, R. W., & Miller, J. A. (1972). Consumer expectations, product performance, and perceived product quality. *Journal of Marketing Research, 9*(February), 19–21.

Parasuraman, A., Zeithaml, V., & Berry, L.L. (1985). A conceptual model of service quality and its implications for future research. *Journal of Marketing, 49*(Autumn), 41–50.

Parasuraman, A., Zeithaml, V., & Berry, L. L. (1988). SERVQUAL: A multiple-item scale for measuring consumer perceptions of service quality. *Journal of Retailing, 64*(Spring), 12–40.

Parasuraman, A., Zeithaml, V., & Berry, L. L. (1991). Refinement and reassessment of the SERVQUAL scale. *Journal of Retailing, 67*(4), 420–450.

Parasuraman, A., Zeithmal, V. A., & Malhotra, A. (2005). E-S-QUAL: A multiple-item scale for assessing electronic service quality. *Journal of Service Research, 7*(3), 213–233.

Patrício, L., Fisk, R. P., Cunha, J. F., & Constantine, L. (2011). Multilevel service design: From customer value constellation to service experience blueprinting. *Journal of Service Research, 14*(2), 180–200.

Pucinelli, N. M., Goodstein, R. C., Grewal, D., Price, R., Raghubir, P., & Stewart, D. (2009). Customer experience management in retailing: Understanding the buying process. *Journal of Retailing, 85*(March), 15–30.

Reichheld, F. F., & Sasser, W. E. Jr (1990). Zero defections: Quality comes to service. *Harvard Business Review*, September–October, 105–111.

Richard, M. D., & Allaway, A. W. (1993). Service quality attributes and choice behavior. *Journal of Services Marketing, 7*(1), 59–68.

Roggeveen, A. L., Tsiros, M., & Grewal, D. (2012). Understanding the co-creation effect: When does collaborating with customers provide a lift to service recovery? *Journal of the Academy of Marketing Science, 40*, 771–790.

Roschk, H., & Gelbrich, K. (2014). Identifying appropriate compensation types for service failures: A meta-analytic and experimental analysis. *Journal of Service Research, 17*(2), 195–211.

Roschk, H., & Gelbrich, K. (2017). Compensation revisited: A social resource theory perspective on offering a monetary resource after a service failure. *Journal of Service Research, 20*(4), 393–408.

Rose, S., Clark, M., Samouel, P., & Hair, N. (2012). Online customer experience in e-retailing: An empirical model of antecedents and outcomes. *Journal of Retailing, 88*(2), 308–322.

Schaefers, T., Wittkowski, K., Benoit, S., & Ferraro, R. (2015). Customer misbehaviour in access-based consumption. *Journal of Service Research, 19*(1), 3–21.

Shaver, P., Schwartz, J., Kirson, D., & O'Connor, C. (1987). Emotion knowledge: Further exploration of a prototype approach. *Journal of Personality and Social Psychology, 52*(6), 1061–1086.

Sheth, J. N., & Parvatiyar, A. (1995). The evolution of relationship marketing. *International Business Review, 4*(4), 397–418.

Shostack, L. (1984). Designing services that deliver. *Harvard Business Review, 62*(1), 133–139.

Singh, J., & Crisafulli, B. (2015). Customer responses to service failure and recovery experiences. In *Boundary Spanning Elements and the Marketing Function in Organizations: Concepts and Empirical Studies*, Sahadev, S. and Purani, K. and Malhotra, N. (Eds.). Cham: Springer (pp. 117–135).

Smith, A. K., Bolton, R. N., & Wagner, J. (1999). A model of customer satisfaction with service encounters involving failure and recovery. *Journal of Marketing Research*, *36*(3), 356–372.

Spanjol, J., Cui. A. S., Nakata, C., Sharp, L. K., Crawford, S. Y., Xiao, Y., & Watson-Manheim, M. B. (2015). Co-production of prolonged, complex, and negative services: An examination of medication adherence in chronically Ill individuals. *Journal of Service Research*, *18*(3), 284–302.

Stroessner, S. J. & Benitez, J. (2019). The social perception of humanoid and non-humanoid robots: Effects of gendered and machinelike features. *International Journal of Social Robotics*, *11*, 305–315.

van Doorn, J., Mende, M., Noble, S. M., Hulland, J., Ostrom, A. L., Grewal, D., & Petersen, J. A. (2017). Domo arigato Mr. Roboto: Emergence of automated social presence in organizational frontlines and customers' service experiences. *Journal of Service Research*, *20*(1), 43–58.

Vanhamme, J., & Grobben, B. (2009). 'Too good to be true!'. The effectiveness of CSR history in countering negative publicity. *Journal of Business Ethics*, *85*(2), 273–283.

Van Vaerenberg, Y., Hazée, S., & Costers, A. (2018). Customer participation in service recovery: A meta-analysis. *Marketing Letters*, *29*, 465–483.

Van Vaerenberg, Y., Varga, D., De Keyser, A., & Orsingher, C. (2019). The service recovery journey: Conceptualization, integration, and directions for future research. *Journal of Service Research*, *22*(2), 103–119.

Vargo, S. L., & Lusch, R. F. (2016). Institutions and axioms: An extension and update of service-dominant logic. *Journal of the Academy of Marketing Science*, 44, 5–23.

Verhoef, P. C., & Lemon, K. N. (2015). Advances in customer value management. In *Handbook on Research in Relationship Marketing*, Morgan, Robert M., Parish, Janet Turner, & Deitz, George (Eds.). Cheltenham: Elgar (pp. 75–103).

Voorhees, C. M., Brady, M. K., & Horowitz, D. M. (2006). A voice from the silent masses: An exploratory and comparative analysis of noncomplainers. *Journal of the Academy of Marketing Science*, *34*(4), 514–527.

Wang, Y. J., Hernandez, M. D., & Minor, M. S. (2010). Web aesthetics effects on perceived online service quality and satisfaction in an e-tail environment: The moderating role of purchase task. *Journal of Business Research*, *63*, 935–942.

Wirtz, J., Kunz, W., & Paluch, S. (2021). The service revolution, intelligent automation and service robots. *European Business Review*, *29*(5), 909.

Wirtz, J., Patterson, P. G., Kunz, W.H., Gruber, T., Lu, V.N., Paluch, S., & Martins, A. (2018). Brave new world: Service robots in the frontline. *Journal of Service Management*, *29*(5), 907–931.

Wünderlich, N. V., von Wangenheim, F., & Bitner, M. J. (2013). High Tech and High Touch: A framework for understanding user attitudes and behaviors related to smart interactive services. *Journal of Service Research*, *16*(1), 3–20.

Yao, T., Zheng, Q., & Fan, X. (2015). The impact of online social support on patients' quality of life and the moderating role of social exclusion. *Journal of Service Research, 18*(3), 369–383.

Zeelenberg, M., & Pieters, R. (2004). Beyond valence in customer dissatisfaction: A review and new findings on behavioral responses to regret and disappointment in failed services. *Journal of Business Research, 57*(4), 445–455.

Zeithaml, V. A., Parasuraman, A., & Berry, L. L. (1985). Problems and strategies in services marketing. *Journal of Marketing, 49*(2), 33–46.

Zhu, Z., Nakata, C. Sivakumar, K., & Grewal, D. (2007). Self-service technology effectiveness: The role of design features and individual traits. *Journal of the Academy of Marketing Science, 35*, 492–506.

Zhu, Z., Nakata, C., Sivakumar, K., & Grewal, D. (2013). Fix it or leave it? Customer Recovery from self-service technology failures. *Journal of Retailing, 89*(1), 15–29.

5 How Consumers Buy Brands

5.1 Introduction

A critical measure of a brand's equity is its market performance. Academic research employing consumer panels owned by companies such as the Kantar Group, Nielsen, GfK, and IRI has documented performance measurement and applications in the management of brands. Consumer panels continuously record purchases of thousands of households, and the data made available by the panels has spurred scholarly research over the past six decades or so, revealing useful insights on how consumers buy their brands. The panels capture brand equity measures such as market share, brand penetration, frequency of purchases, share of category requirements and the proportion of light and heavy buyers. Seminal research in domain suggests that most mature consumer markets are approximately stationary (i.e., brand sales change little from year to year). Research on stationarity has revealed patterns in the data that show a law-like regularity, and the findings remain stable across product categories, services, business-to-business markets, subscription markets and countries.

This chapter provides an overview of the empirical generalisations tradition in marketing, the measurement of brand performance and the role of theory in understanding brand buying behaviour. The chapter illustrates the breadth of 60+ years of robust empirical evidence in the domain. It ends with a discussion of recent research advances and applications, and the implications for future research.

5.2 Empirical Generalisations in Marketing

The developments in marketing research have been much influenced by explanations of different types of phenomena that can be generalised across different conditions. These phenomena, which are known as

DOI: 10.4324/9780429449598-5

the empirical generalisations, are now considered integral to our understanding of buyer behaviour and form a basis for reusable knowledge in marketing. A significant development in this field concerns the body of knowledge developed by Professor Andrew Ehrenberg and his colleagues who have extensively researched customer purchase data. They discovered patterns of buyer behaviour that can be generalised across a range of product categories.

In marketing literature, studies based on empirical generalisations are few. Bass (1995) defines empirical generalisations as a pattern or regularity that repeats over different circumstances and that can be described simply by mathematical, graphic or symbolic methods. This pattern repeats but may not be universal over all circumstances. More generally, these are patterns or regularities that occur over different circumstances and which therefore are amenable to mathematical, graphical, or symbolic representation. Ehrenberg (1988) suggests that the law-like relationships of science are descriptive generalisations. They are also the building blocks of higher level theory and explanation.

The law-like relationships have the following properties:

- They are of limited generality rather than universal.
- They are approximate rather than exact.
- They are not necessarily derived from theory.
- They are broadly descriptive rather than causal.

Barwise (1995) adds a different perspective to the discussion with his listing of five characteristics of a good empirical generalisation: scope, precision, parsimony, usefulness and link with theory. Ehrenberg (1993) advocates the use of replication studies across multiple sets of data covering a wide range of conditions to establish the scope of empirical generalisations. Empirical generalisations can be seen as the building blocks of scientific knowledge. The idea of using multiple sets of data is, therefore, central to producing generalisable results that lead to empirically grounded theory. A summary of some prominent empirical generalisations in marketing and the approaches employed to generate empirical generalisations are illustrated in Table 5.1.

Scholars concur that empirical generalisations lead to robust marketing research tradition. The concept has been extended to investigate different aspects of consumer behaviour even though the studies seem to differ in their methodologies and goals. Blattberg et al. (1995), for example, have analysed the empirical generalisations related to sales promotion by looking at the effects of this marketing tool across multiple studies. The authors hold that empirical generalisations are

Table 5.1 Illustrative Empirical Generalisations in Marketing

Subject	Author/Authors	Generalisations
Diffusion	Bass	The Bass Model and extensions such as the extension to multiple generations of technologies are empirical generalisations.
	Mahajan, Muller, Bass	The conditional probability of adoption at time $T = p + QF(T)$ (the Bass Model) and thus the adoption rate depends upon the number of previous adopters.
Choice	Ehrenberg	The Dirichlet distribution describes the repeat buying and brand-switching behaviour of consumers.
	Uncles, Ehrenberg, Hammond	Each consumer habitually buys from a small set of brands, with steady long-run propensities or probabilities of buying. brand choices are independent of the brand bought last (implying a zero-order process).
	Meyer, Johnson	Attribute valuations are nonlinear and reference dependent.
Market Response (short-run)	Ehrenberg, Bijmolt et al., Hanssens	The price elasticity for closely substitutable brands is –2.6.
	Farley, Lehmann, Sawyer	Meta-analysis indicates price elasticities of about –2, advertising elasticities of 0.25 and elasticities of buyer behaviour models about 0.3.

Source: Adapted from Bass (1995).

essential to the development of theoretical results. Similarly, Dekimpe and Hanssens (1995) derive a number of empirical generalisations about conditions under which markets are likely to evolve, concluding that generalisations provide a foundation for the study of long-run marketing effectiveness. While several such studies (e.g., Kalyanaram et al., 1995; Kaul & Wittink, 1995; Mahajan et al., 1995; Reibstein & Farris, 1995) attempt to find generalisable results, most are isolated studies and without any follow-up research. This lack of validation through further studies has, to some extent, impeded the development of theory which is empirically sound, as pointed out by Blattberg et al. (1995). Given that the results are not tested or validated, their generalisability remains unclear. In this regard, Hanssens (2018) suggests that, from a theoretical perspective, single case studies can be generally sufficient, as these serve as illustrations of broader principles that are the focus of academic enquiry. However, from a managerial perspective, studies with a single set of data may be considered anecdotal in nature as the business manager might want to know, for instance, whether or not a planned communications campaign will have a productive impact across the sector.

Advocating the use of meta-analysis, Hanssens (2018) further suggests that combining the results of dozens or hundreds of comparable studies may reveal a replicable pattern in the data, which forms the basis of an empirical generalisation that is highly informative to the decision-makers. Previously, Farley et al. (1995) have illustrated how meta-analysis has produced empirical generalisations concerning parameters in models of advertising, price, diffusion and consumer behaviour. Using the results of 1851 published price response estimates, Bijmolt et al. (2005) conclude that average brand-level price elasticities are −2.62, and Albers et al. (2010), on the other hand, collected 506 sales call response estimates to derive that sales call elasticities average to 0.31. Similarly, a special issue in the *Journal of Advertising Research* (2009, volume 49, issue 2), showcases 23 empirical generalisations in advertising. Further such studies are needed towards bridging the current gap between academic research and managerial practice.

5.3 Brand Performance Metrics/Measures

The two main measures of loyalty are market share and the market penetration of a brand. Market share denotes the percentage of total category sales the brand accounts for. The penetration of an item is the proportion of population who buy the item at least once in a given time period. Penetration is also denoted as b_x for item x. Although the two measures are expressed as percentages, they differ both conceptually and arithmetically:

$$Market\text{-}share = \frac{\text{Total purchases of the brand } \%}{\text{Total purchases of the category}}$$

$$Penetration = \frac{\text{The number buying the brand at least once } \%}{\text{The total number of potential customers}}$$

The relationship between market share and penetration is that they vary closely together. It is also observed that the difference between the values of the penetration between two brands can be large while the difference in their respective average purchase frequency is of smaller magnitude.

5.3.1 Purchase Frequency

The average purchase frequency is the average number of purchases made by households who buy at all in a given period. This figure hardly varies regardless of the size of the brand, although purchase frequency tends to be slightly lower for smaller brands. McPhee (1963) label this phenomenon as 'Double Jeopardy', whereby smaller brands are bought by fewer people (lower penetration) and they are bought less often (lower average purchase frequency). McPhee (1963) demonstrates that theoretically Double Jeopardy is a statistical selection effect that occurs because of the differences in market share among competing brands. It is now a well-established trend observed for a wide variety of packaged goods categories and has been documented in many contexts (e.g., brands and stores, developed and emerging economies, product variants, new brands (see also Dall'Olmo Riley et al., 1997; Ehrenberg et al., 1990; Ehrenberg et al., 2004; Singh et al., 2012; Uncles & Hammond, 1995; Uncles & Kwok, 2009; Uncles et al., 2010).

5.3.2 100%-Loyal Buyers

Most customers buy a product from many different brands. There is a group of customers, however, who buy only one single brand of a certain product category throughout the time period of analysis. These are called the 100%-loyals or the sole buyers of a brand. The 100%-loyal buyers or the sole buyers are low for all the brands, irrespective of their market shares. This trend affirms multi-brand buying behaviour.

5.3.3 Share of Category Requirements

Share of category requirements is one of the most commonly used measures of brand loyalty. It measures each brand's market share among the group of householders that bought the brand at least once during the time period under consideration.

Thus, the share of average buyer's total requirements over a period, that are accounted for by a specific brand equals to

> average purchase frequency per buyer for a brand during the period
>
> ―――――――――――――――――――――――――――――――――――
>
> total amount of product category bought in a period by buyers of a brand

The share of category requirements for most brands is low.

5.3.4 Heavy Buyers

Those buying five times or more are classified as heavy buyers. Bigger brands have more buyers who bought the brand more often, due to the popularity of the brand. The incidence of heavy buyers follows a downward trend with market share.

5.3.5 Light Buyers

Those customers who bought the brand once during the time period are classified as light buyers. In general, there is a high percentage of customers buying a brand only once over a period of time. Generally smaller brands have a bigger proportion of once-only buyers.

5.3.6 Duplication of Purchase

Since only some customers of a brand tend to be 100%-loyal in a chosen analysis period, other customers of a brand tend to switch easily and revert to the purchase of other brands. The levels of switching are commonly interpreted in terms of which brands are more or less competitive with each other. Buying X and then Y need not mean that the consumer is totally giving up brand X in favour of brand Y but may have both X and Y in their ongoing brand repertoire (i.e., set of preferred brands in any one product category). This phenomenon is known as Brand Duplication of Purchase, which shows the number of purchasers of a brand who also purchase in the same period another brand (i.e., buyers of brand X also buy brand Y). The analysis is carried out on the number of buyers, rather than the number or volume of purchases. The duplication results reveal that most buyers are regularly switching between brands in a repertoire, and such a behaviour is not necessarily indicative of how competitive brands are.

5.4 How Theory Explains Brand Loyalty

Generalised empirical research findings have a strong link with theory, as shown is an influential and substantive stream of research spanning more than six decades. The Negative Binomial Distribution (NBD)-Dirichlet model of choice behaviour in competitive market situations provides that link and substantiates empirical generalisations (Ehrenberg et al., 2004; Goodhardt et al., 1984; Wind & Sharp, 2009). The Dirichlet is a descriptive model first developed in mathematics, then applied in different disciplines, including marketing. Ehrenberg and his colleagues have established that how often people buy a product and the brands or products that they buy is largely habitual, with individual behaviour aggregating to measures of brand performance which follows regular law-like patterns (e.g., Ehrenberg et al., 2004; Sharp et al., 2012; Singh et al., 2008). The finding that most markets behave in a predictable 'Dirichlet' manner has led to the conclusion that:

a   Loyalty (the propensity to purchase) at the individual consumer level has multiple causes. It produces a common effect at the brand level, which is captured by many different measures.
b   Competing brands differ little in the levels of loyalty they enjoy.

The Dirichlet model is used to predict a range of brand output measures related to loyalty, and these can all be predicted from the market share of a brand. Apart from this brand-specific input, the Dirichlet model also requires information on the penetration and purchase frequency of the total product category and a specified length for the analysis period as inputs. The *observed* patterns in real purchase data extracted from consumer panels are closely benchmarked against the patterns *predicted* by the Dirichlet model. The evidence shows that when a market is stationary, the predicted estimates for brand performance measures, such as repeat purchase, share of category requirement, the relative number of heavy and light buyers and the pattern of cross-brand buying in a category (purchase duplication), are very closely aligned with the observed estimates at any given amount of time.

Panel data on routine consumer purchases show that in the medium to long-term, most markets are mature or established. Market stationarity occurs because of the competitive market structure, where several brands are competing for market shares. This is the bedrock of the stationary market theory. A key feature of these markets is that they usually do not change much in terms of the market shares of the brands. Markets may change over short periods because of sales promotions, but usually these gains are not maintained when the promotion ends (Ehrenberg & England, 1990; Ehrenberg et al., 1994; Ehrenberg et al., 2004, Uncles et al., 2012). Given that price-based promotions run for short periods of time, the gains these marketing efforts produce have little effect when averaged over several months, and are counter-balanced when competitors run promotions. As a result, the market remains stable over a period of several months or a year.

Early seminal research on brand modelling by Ehrenberg (e.g., papers in 1959, 1969) has been later brought together in a book entitled *Repeat Buying: Theory and Applications* (Ehrenberg, 1988). The book challenges conventional beliefs in marketing and encourages the reappraisal of some of the traditional ideas about brand loyalty, brand positioning, the effects of advertising and the way in which sales grow. It has been followed by work in the United States investigating the mathematical properties of stationary market models. Morrison and Schmittlein (1981, 1988), for example, give detailed attention to the models and any modifications that can improve their precision. Mathematical models can also be applied to other forms of stable repetitive behaviour. Goodhardt et al. (1975) used such a model to study television audiences. Another application concerns store choice, with store groups being treated as brands (Kau & Ehrenberg, 1984; Wright et al., 1998). It is also possible to model other category divisions such as a pack size (Singh et al., 2008).

The systematic study of the brand performance metrics has led to generalisable patterns as summarised below:

- Brand penetrations vary within a product category and are much lower for smaller brands.
- Average buying frequencies do not vary much amongst brands in a category. Underlying these averages, some individuals are heavy buyers and others are light buyers.
- Smaller brands not only have fewer buyers than larger brands, but buyers of smaller brands also buy the brand slightly less often than do buyers of bigger brands – the so-called Double Jeopardy effect.
- 100%-loyal buyers are relatively rare – in one year, almost all buyers of a typical brand are multi-brand buyers and divided in their loyalty.

- Levels of loyalty are higher in shorter instead of lengthier periods of time, mainly because there are fewer opportunities to purchase different brands.
- Most buyers of a brand also buy other brands leading to the duplication of purchase, which correlates with brand penetration.

The above patterns are observed in the raw data and are also closely predictable from the Dirichlet model. Major exceptions from the Dirichlet's predictions are noticeably uncommon, although there may be minor exceptions or deviations from the model's predictions. In many cases, the exceptions are simply explicable as one-off events (e.g., a serious stock-out or disruption because of weather conditions, a strike or fire in the warehouse) or statistical anomalies (e.g., with small brands the underlying consumer sample might be small, leading to a statistical sampling effect).

Empirical research on stationary markets describes *how* consumers buy mutually competing brands. Stationary market research, however, does not explain *why* some people buy more than others and one brand rather than another. Some critics argue that the lack of attention to such motivational issues limits the application of these models, particularly when the marketer is trying to induce behavioural change. Stationary market researchers exclude motivation and attitudes in their examination of purchase data. By contrast, the focus is on the patterns of purchase in stable markets, which is the nature of most markets, and the numerical predictions from the model are usually very close to the observations derived from panel data. When the market is not stationary (e.g., a new category is introduced), the difference between the observed facts and the model predictions can help to understand the way the market is changing.

5.5 Applications in Marketing

The empirically generalisable findings from brand purchase data across several product categories, countries, time span and contexts have applications in brand management. The main patterns of buyer behaviour are summarised below.

- In practice, loyalty patterns are dominated by how big each brand is (i.e., its market share) and not, or hardly, by any idiosyncratic attributes or characteristics of a brand.
- The buying of particular products and brands is largely habitual and an important reason for this is that consumers themselves are

mostly already highly experienced in terms of buying propensities for the brands they regularly buy.

- People form personal repertoires of perhaps three or four brands from which they habitually choose one brand more often than others (e.g., a consumer may have a repertoire of three brands, with long-run propensities to buy these brands 60%, 30% and 10% of the time).
- Within such a framework of mostly steady, but divided loyalties, individual purchases are made in an apparently irregular or even 'as-if-random' manner, although with underlying reasons (i.e., there will be underlying individual needs and preferences, as well as the effects of availability and other situational factors, prices and promotions, but the behavioural outcome may appear to be random).

The Dirichlet framework offers numerous practical uses, such as auditing the performance of established brands, predicting the performance of new brands, checking the nature of unfamiliar or partitioned or dynamic markets, assessing the impact of advertising and promotions. The applications are the cornerstones of buyer behaviour and provide direction to the brand manager:

- The brand should aim to get into more people's repertoires – building reach rather than being concerned about securing exclusive loyalty.
- The brand should aim to match its competitor's advantages and position itself as a good example of a product offering in the category.
- Customers have direct experience of the brand, therefore encouraging distinctive memory traces could be useful.
- The brand should appeal to all customers in a market, not just specific, narrow segments.
- The brand should be circumspect about price-based promotions, as these might only attract existing customers, not new ones.
- Brand advertising should remind buyers of its continued existence and availability, and 'tell a good story well'.
- The brand should defend its market share, considering that even a big brand has several brands competing against it.

5.6 Recent Research Advances

Recent research advances in the domain include the debate between differentiation and distinctiveness, the notion of mental availability, benchmarking new brand buyer behaviour, and above all, the Dirichlet model applications. Below is an overview of key research publications advancing knowledge on how consumers buy their brands.

Examining grocery purchase data at brand level (Kantar Worlwide Panel, UK), Romaniuk and Sharp (2016) show that the Double Jeopardy trend applies for both online and offline buying. In the fashion retail category, online shoppers' behaviour looks similar to the behaviour of bricks-and-mortar shoppers. The authors report slightly higher incidence of online as compared with offline loyalty, citing empirical research by Dawes and Nencyz-Thiel (2013, 2014). Overall, the online loyalty patterns shows repertoire buying, namely buyers buy from a repertoire, or basket, of brands with patterns that can be predicted given market share estimates. In a similar vein, Trinh et al. (2017) investigate online buying behaviour of supermarket consumers over time, and find that the model provides good fit. Likewise, using the Dirichlet model, Chowdhury et al. (2022) model how fashion brands compete in an online auction platform—an essential extension of established offline patterns to an important online domain. Naami et al. (2022) extend knowledge in e-loyalty and apply duplication of purchase analysis to online purchases for multiple digital markets in the geographical context of Iran, the fastest-growing e-commerce market in the Middle East, further establishing the applications in the digital domains.

The multi-brand buying patterns reported in prior studies are also observed in the services sector (e.g., Dawes et al., 2009; Mundt et al., 2006; Sharp et al., 2002). The evidence suggests that despite the investments in customer relationship management and cross-selling activities, brands do not outperform their direct competitors in terms of cross-category loyalty in their respective markets (Mundt et al., 2006). In the domain of luxury, Romaniuk and Sharp (2016) report that luxury brands compete similarly to non-luxury brands. The authors find evidence for the duplication of purchase law, wherein buyers of a luxury brand buy other luxury brands in proportion to the brand's penetration. A luxury brand might share its buyers with other luxury brands, more so with large brands and less so with small brands.

Singh and Dall'Olmo Riley (2022) use the model to investigate consumer perceived differences in branded commodities, an aspect that is surprisingly under-researched and poorly understood in managerial practice. The study investigates consumers' perceived differentiation of commodity brands (e.g., rice, petrol, salt, water). Using data from three countries, across four commodity categories, the study examines consumers' brand/attribute associations, brand commitment and loyalty-related brand performance measures are benchmarked against the output from the Dirichlet model. Overall, the results show that the commodity brands follow the Dirichlet-type empirical patterns. The model's implications extend beyond consumer buying behaviour into the field of advertising and media research. This is shown by Graham and Kennedy (2022) who project the Dirichlet model estimates over the long term to quantify buyers of consumer goods brands for advertisers. Results demonstrate that the customer base (brand penetration) must increase substantially over time to maintain, let alone grow, market share. The analysis over a five years period shows that more than a third of brand buyers buy the brand just once, and such buyers are vital to sales and critical to growth.

The duplication of purchase law continues to be applied widely across sectors and contexts. Applying the Dirichlet model in the capital goods industry, Wilkinson et al. (2016) show that the duplication of purchase describes buying behaviour for industrial purchases. The authors show a good NBD fit, along with the successful application of the conditional trend analysis, in line with estimates from previously studied industrial markets. In the wine market, Wilson and Winchester (2019) explore the applicability of recognised generalisations to the European wine retail market. The authors show that consumer wine repurchase follows a double jeopardy pattern and the duplication of purchase law. Adding a novel dimension to the duplication of purchase research, Anesbury et al. (2022) show that market partitions exist not only over the short term or annual data as previous studies established, but persist over the long term (i.e., three years). In another interesting application, Wilson et al. (2019) apply the above theoretical precepts to exercise behaviour, terming it the duplication of behaviour law. The authors demonstrate that population-level patterns of behaviour can yield insight into the competition between different activities, and show how engagement in physical activity is shared across different exercise and sport activities. Such insights can be used to describe and predict physical activity behaviour and may be used to inform and evaluate promotional messages and policy intervention. Further applications are by Mecredy et al. (2022) who examine two crucial drivers of consumer behaviour: brand awareness and brand consideration through the lens of duplication of purchase and double jeopardy. They show that brands with low recognition suffer twice as much as brands with high recognition given lower unaided brand recall and lower purchase consideration. The authors confirm the existence of duplication of awareness and duplication of consideration patterns, wherein brands share greater awareness or consideration levels with other highly recognised or considered brands, than with less recognised brands. Similarly, studies by Anesbury et al. (2022) and Grasby et al. (2022) extend the framework into studying the persistence of partitions in duplication of purchase, and loyalty to brand extensions across categories. The above studies are exciting advancements in the domain and show the endurance of the empirical generalisations and the robust Dirichlet-type buyer behaviour. The findings have direct applications in marketing practice and are immensely important for bridging the gap between academic research and practice in marketing.

The prominence of data-driven marketing has led to considerable effort in marketing to gather, store, process and interpret ever-larger quantities of data, often resulting in the use of complex decision-support systems (Zhao et al., 2009). This can be a daunting prospect, but employing the well-established structure provided in a Dirichlet framework offers a starting point; the digital footprint of customers can be trawled through, and patterns identified to understand the online browsing, reading and buying behaviour in sources of large-scale data. For instance, Chan and Uncles (2022) focus on *dashboards* which are commonly used to inform data-driven decision-making, using the Dirichlet model to construct coherent and integrated dashboards. This is demonstrated using an example that offers guidance to practitioners and researchers for incorporating the model into a dashboard. The model allows enhanced visualisation, communication, and decision-making. The authors also show the applicability of the model in analysing a non-brand attribute, specifically magazine content sections, which are read by consumers in patterns that follow the double jeopardy principle. Such innovative application in a new context suggests the continuing applications and benefits of the Dirichlet framework.

References

Albers, S., Mantrala, M. K., & Sridhar, S. (2010). Personal selling elasticities: A meta-analysis. *Journal of Marketing Research*, *47*(5), 840–853.

Anesbury, Z. W., Bennett, D., & Kennedy, R. (2022). How persistent are duplication of purchase partitions? *Journal of Consumer Behaviour*, *21*(1), 137–152.

Barwise, P. (1995). Good empirical generalisations. *Marketing Science*, *14*(3), Part 2 of 2.

Bass, F. (1995). Empirical generalisations and marketing science: A personal view. *Marketing Science*, *14*(3), G6–G19.

Bijmolt, T. H. A., van Heerde, H. J., & Pieters, R. G. M. (2005). New empirical generalizations on the determinants of price elasticity. *Journal of Marketing Research*, *42*(2), 141–156.

Blattberg, R. C., Briesch R., & Fox, E. J. (1995). How promotions work. *Marketing Science, 14*(3), G122–G132.

Chan, K., & Uncles, M. (2022). Digital media consumption: Using metrics, patterns and dashboards to enhance data-driven decision-making. *Journal of Consumer Behaviour, 21*(1), 80–91.

Chowdhury, S., Barker, A., Trinh, G., & Lockshin, L. (2022). Using the Dirichlet model to predict how fashion brands compete and grow on eBay. *Journal of Consumer Behaviour, 21*(1), 63–79.

Dawes, J., Mundt, K., & Sharp, B. (2009). Consideration sets for financial services brands. *Journal of Financial Services Marketing, 14*(3), 190–202.

Dawes, J. & Nenycz-Thiel, M. (2013). Analyzing the intensity of private label competition across retailers. *Journal of Business Research, 66*(1), 60–66.

Dawes, J. & Nenycz-Thiel, M. (2014). Comparing retailer purchase patterns and brand metrics for in-store and online grocery purchasing. *Journal of Marketing Management, 30*(3–4): 364–382.

Dekimpe, M. & Hanssens, D. (1995). Empirical generalisations about market evolution and stationarity. *Marketing Science, 14*(3), G109–121.

Ehrenberg, A. S. (1959). The pattern of consumer purchases. *Journal of the Royal Statistical Society: Series C (Applied Statistics), 8*(1), 26–41.

Ehrenberg, A. S. (1969). Towards an integrated theory of consumer behaviour. *Journal of the Market Research Society, 11*(4), 305–337.

Ehrenberg, A. S. C (1972/1988). *Repeat-Buying: Facts, Theory and Applications* (1st and 2nd editions). London; Griffin; New York: Oxford University Press.

Ehrenberg, A. S. (1994). Theory or well-based results: which comes first?. In *Research traditions in marketing* (pp. 79–131). Springer, Dordrecht.

Ehrenberg, A. S. C., & England, L. R. (1990). Generalising a pricing effect. *The Journal of Industrial Economics, 39*(1), 47–68.

Ehrenberg, A. S. C., Goodhardt, G. J., & Barwise, T. P. (1990). Double jeopardy revisited. *Journal of Marketing, 54*(3), 82–91.

Ehrenberg, A. S. C., Goodhardt, G. J., & Collins, M. (1975). The way that people watch television. *New Society*, 262–263.

Ehrenberg, A. S.C, Hammond, K., & Goodhart, G. J. (1994). The after-effects of price-related consumer promotions. *Journal of advertising Research, 34*(4), 11–22.

Ehrenberg, A. S. C., Uncles, M. D., & Goodhardt, G. J. (2004). Understanding brand performance measures: Using Dirichlet benchmarks. *Journal of Business Research, 57*(12), 1307–1325.

Farley, J., Lehmann D, & Sawyer, A. (1995). Empirical marketing generalisation using meta-analysis, *Marketing Science, 14*(3), Part 2 of 2.

Goodhardt, G. J., Ehrenberg, A. S. C., & Chatfield, C. (1984). The Dirichlet: A comprehensive model of buying behaviour. *Journal of the Royal Statistical Society A, 147*, 621–655.

Graham, C., & Kennedy, R. (2022). Quantifying the target market for advertisers. *Journal of Consumer Behaviour, 21*(1), 33–48.

Grasby, A., Corsi, A., Dawes, J., Driesener, C., & Sharp, B. (2022). How loyalty extends across product categories. *Journal of Consumer Behaviour, 21*(1), 153–163.

Hanssens, D. M. (2018). The value of empirical generalizations in marketing. *Journal of the Academy of Marketing Science, 46*(1), 6–8

Kalyanaram, G., Robinson, W., & Urban, G. (1995). Order of market entry: Established empirical generalisations, emerging empirical generalisations, and future research. *Marketing Science, 14*(3), G161–169.

Kau, A. K. & Ehrenberg, A. S. C. (1984). Patterns of store choice. *Journal of Marketing Research, 21*, 99–409.

Kaul, A. & Wittink, D. (1995). Empirical generalisations about the impact of advertising on price sensitivity and price. *Marketing Science, 14*(3), G151–160.

Mahajan, V., Muller, E. & Bass, F. (1995). Diffusion of new products: Empirical generalisations and managerial uses. *Marketing Science, 14*(3), G79–G88.

Mcphee, W. N. (1963). *Formal Theories of Mass Behaviour.* Glencoe, IL: Free Press.

Mecredy, P. J., Wright, M. J., Feetham, P. M., & Stern, P. (2022). Empirical generalisations in customer mindset metrics. *Journal of Consumer Behaviour, 21*(1), 102–120.

Morrison, D. G., & Schmittlein, D. C. (1981). Predicting future random events based on past performance. *Management Science, 27*(9), 1006–1023.

Morrison, D. G. & Schmittlein, D. C. (1988). Generalizing the NBD model for customer purchases: What are the implications and is it worth the effort? *Journal of Business and Economic Statistics, 6*, 145–166.

Mundt, K., Dawes, J., & Sharp, B. (2006). Can a brand outperform competitors on cross-category loyalty? An examination of cross-selling metrics in two financial services markets. *Journal of Consumer Marketing, 23*(7), 465–469.

Naami, T., Anesbury, Z. W., Stocchi, L., & Winchester, M. (2022). How websites compete in the Middle East: The example of Iran. *Journal of Consumer Behaviour, 21*(1), 121–136.

Reibstein, D. & P. Farris (1995). Market share and distribution: A generalisation, a speculation and some implications. *Marketing Science, 14*(3), G190–202.

Riley, F. D. O., Ehrenberg, A. S. C., Castleberry, S. B., & Barwise, T. P. (1997). The variability of attitudinal repeat-rates. *International Journal of Research in Marketing, 14*(5), 437–450.

Sharp, B., & Romaniuk, J. (2016). *How Brands Grow.* England: Oxford University Press.

Sharp, B., Wright, M., Dawes, J., Driesener, C., Meyer-Waarden, L., Stocchi, L., & Stern, P. (2012). It's a Dirichlet world: Modeling individuals' loyalties reveals how brands compete, grow, and decline. *Journal of Advertising Research, 52*(2), 203–213.

Sharp, B., Wright, M., & Goodhardt, G. (2002). Purchase loyalty is polarised into either repertoire or subscription patterns. *Australasian Marketing Journal, 10*(3), 7–20.

Singh, J., & Dall'Olmo Riley, F. (2022). Consumer perceptions and behaviour towards branded commodities. *Journal of Consumer Behaviour*, *21*(1), 19–32.

Singh, J., Ehrenberg, A., & Goodhardt, G. (2008). Measuring customer loyalty to product variants. *International Journal of Market Research*, *50*(4), 513–532.

Singh, J., Scriven, J., Clemente, M., Lomax, W., & Wright, M. (2012). New brand extensions: Patterns of success and failure. *Journal of Advertising Research*, *52*(2), 234–242.

Trinh, G. T., Anesbury, Z. W., & Driesener, C. (2017). Has behavioural loyalty to online supermarkets declined? *Australasian Marketing Journal*, *25*(4), 326–333.

Uncles, M., & Hammond, K. (1995). Grocery store patronage. *International Review of Retail, Distribution and Consumer Research*, *5*(3), 287–302.

Uncles, M., Kennedy, R., Nenycz-Thiel, M., Singh, J., & Kwok, S. (2012). In 25 years, across 50 categories, user profiles for directly competing brands seldom differ: Affirming Andrew Ehrenberg's principles. *Journal of Advertising Research*, *52*(2), 252–261.

Uncles, M. D., & Kwok, S. (2009). Patterns of store patronage in urban China. *Journal of Business Research*, *62*(1), 68–81.

Uncles, M. D., Wang, C., & Kwok, S. (2010). A temporal analysis of behavioural brand loyalty among urban Chinese consumers. *Journal of Marketing Management*, *26*(9–10), 921–942.

Wilkinson, J. W., Trinh, G., Lee, R., & Brown, N. (2016). Can the negative binomial distribution predict industrial purchases? *Journal of Business & Industrial Marketing*, *31*(4), 543–552.

Wilson, A. L., Nguyen, C., Bogomolova, S., Sharp, B., & Olds, T. (2019). Analysing how physical activity competes: A cross-disciplinary application of the duplication of Behaviour Law. *International Journal of Behavioral Nutrition and Physical Activity*, *16*(1), 1–13.

Wilson, D., & Winchester, M. (2019). Extending the double jeopardy and duplication of purchase laws to the wine market. *International Journal of Wine Business Research*, *31*(2), 163–179.

Wind, Y. J., & Sharp, B. (2009). Advertising empirical generalizations: Implications for research and action. *Journal of Advertising Research*, *49*(2), 246–252.

Wright, M., Sharp, A., & Sharp, B. (1998). Are Australasian brands different? *Journal of Product & Brand Management*, *7*(6), 465–480.

Zhao, L., Uncles, M. D., Gregory, G., Ohsawa, Y., & Yada, K. (2009). *The Use of Online Market Analysis Systems to Achieve Competitive Advantage*. Boca Raton, FL: Chapman & Hall/CRC Data Mining & Knowledge Discovery Series, and Taylor & Francis Group (pp. 35–56).

6 Brand Partnerships

6.1 Introduction

An important development in branding literature pertains to partnerships between two brands, termed co-branding or brand alliance. The strategy refers to various forms of co-operation between two or more brands including joint-sales promotions (e.g., Volvo and Legoland), advertising alliances (e.g., Sony and Ericsson), bundling (e.g., HP and McAfee), ingredient branding (e.g., Apple Pay and Mastercard), and dual branding (e.g., Avis and Budget). Brand alliances have attracted considerable research interest, supported by a substantial number of empirical studies across various contexts, published since the mid-1990s (e.g., Helmig et al., 2008; Kalafatis et al., 2012; Lafferty et al., 2004; Park et al., 1996; Singh, 2016; Singh et al., 2020a, b). Academic research interest in co-branding reflects a growing awareness that leveraging a firm through brand associations is more cost-effective and less risky than traditional brand extension strategies (Besharat & Langan, 2014; Pinello et al., 2022). Furthermore, this approach presents a fresh opportunity for strategic advantage in a competitive marketplace (Bucklin & Sengupta, 1993; Desai & Keller, 2002; Turan, 2021).

Given that co-branding is now a well-established domain of research, a delineation of the different streams of literature with a focus on the factors that drive co-branding success and failure can advance understanding on the subject. A review of the existing knowledge on co-branding could enable both researchers and managers to assess the opportunities as well as the boundaries of introducing and sustaining a cobrand alliance. This chapter presents a state-of-the-art review of the research evidence on co-branding. The review also differentiates the various types of co-branding strategies, and highlights advances in co-branding research in the B2B domain.

DOI: 10.4324/9780429449598-6

6.2 Benefits and Drivers of Co-branding

Several co-branding studies have shown a range of benefits accruing to the partner brands. For instance, an organisation's access to new markets is enhanced when entering a cobrand alliance (Abbratt & Motlana, 2000). Similarly, Vaidyanathan and Aggarwal (2000) affirm that the probability of entry by an unfamiliar brand partnering with a nationally branded ingredient brand is higher when compared to the probability of entry by a new co-branded product without a nationally branded ingredient partner. When an unknown brand partners with a highly reputable one, consumers assume that the overall quality of the product is good because the reputable brand signals quality (Kalafatis et al., 2012; Rao et al., 1999; Singh et al., 2014). In addition to enhancing market access, alliances lower investment in manufacturing, retailing and promotion, all operations that invariably impact price competitiveness (Lambe et al., 2002). Research has also found that co-branding has an effect on revenue generation and cost benefits. Erevelles et al. (2008) suggest that by reducing the probability of entry by competitors, both the manufacturer and supplier brands in an alliance can gain from cost benefits.

Furthermore, research shows that long-term consumers build affective commitment and brand loyalty for the partner brands (Das & Teng, 1998; Fullerton, 2003). In examining the behavioural impact of a co-branded product across segments of consumers with varying levels of brand commitment or loyalty, Swaminathan et al. (2012) show that co-branding can enhance brand sales and overall market share without cannibalising the sales of individual brands. Similarly, Erevelles et al. (2008) suggest that brand alliances with advertising support can enhance the marketing and promotion of the product in the business-to-business context. Such support is likely to increase product awareness, which can lead to an increase in consumer demand and turnover. Other research has shown that co-branding strengthens the brand's competitive position in the marketplace (e.g., Besharat, 2010; Newmeyer et al., 2014). Studies in different sectors show that co-branding can maximise brand value by increasing the equity of the constituent brands in the alliance (e.g., Tasci & Guillet, 2011; Washburn et al., 2004). On the other hand, Washburn et al. (2000) show that although low-equity brands may benefit most from cobranding, high-equity brands are not depreciated even when paired with a low-equity partner. The authors demonstrate that positive product trial increases brand equity for all cobranded combinations. The above finding is supported by Leuthesser et al.

(2003) postulating that powerful brands have relatively little to lose in co-branded ventures, even when the partner brand is weak. However, Lebar et al. (2005) demonstrate that established brands have a higher risk of losing their brand esteem by partnering with an unfamiliar partner. Arnett et al. (2010) show that brand equity of the partner brands could impact behavioural and attitudinal outcomes (e.g., see also Dutta & Pullig, 2011; Koschate-Fischer et al., 2019). In another study concerning brand equity, Kalafatis et al. (2012) suggest that brands with equivalent equity levels share the benefits of the cobranding equally, while lower equity brands benefitting more from the alliance than higher equity partners. Similarly, Kalafatis et al. (2016) show that in the higher education context, a lower-ranking institution can benefit from entering an alliance with a higher-ranked institution.

The above evidence suggests that co-branding with a high-equity brand is a fruitful strategy for a low-equity brand. Overall, the overwhelming amount of evidence points to a range of benefits of the strategy. Co-branding is an alternative brand expansion strategy that can offer benefits to the partnering brands. Further empirical research could examine the assertions that two brands harnessed together can translate into quicker returns, price premiums, access to leading-edge technology and reinforced advertising messages (e.g., Nguyen et al., 2018).

Prior studies have identified the determinants of consumer attitudes towards brand alliances, including consumer awareness of the partner brands (Park et al., 1996), perceived quality of the brands (Rao & Ruekert, 1994; Rao et al., 1999), brand equity (Kalafatis et al., 2012; Vaidyanathan & Aggarwal, 2000; Washburn et al., 2000), positioning strategies (Singh et al., 2014) and existing consumer attitudes towards the partner brands (e.g., Bouten et al., 2011; Lafferty et al., 2004; Simonin & Ruth, 1998). In addition, a substantial amount of research has established that brand fit and product fit have a significant and positive impact on consumer attitudes towards co-branded alliances (e.g., Baumgarth, 2004; Helmig et al., 2007; Moon & Sprott, 2016; Simonin & Ruth, 1998; Singh et al., 2014). Brand fit is the congruence of consumer associations about the partner brands, whereas product fit captures the consumer perception of the similarity and compatibility between two product categories (e.g., Ahn et al., 2020; Bouten et al., 2011; Senechal et al., 2014). Some empirical studies report the primacy of brand image fit over product fit in positive evaluations of the alliance (e.g., Baumgarth, 2004; Simonin & Ruth, 1998). In a notable study, Singh (2016) establish that a new form of fit, called the CSR fit, leads to positive business outcomes. Similarly, Ahn et al. (2020) show the positive influence of perceived sensory fit, which denotes the congruence of colour, shape or size of the partner products, on co-brand evaluation. Brand familiarity, or accumulated knowledge about the brand, also positively influences consumer information processing and brand evaluation (e.g., Lafferty et al., 2004; Naidoo & Hollebeek, 2016). In addition, several studies have established brand trust, namely consumers' confidence in the brand to perform its promised function, as having a positive effect on consumers' purchase intention (e.g., Chaudhuri & Holbrook, 2001; Kalafatis et al., 2016, Naido & Hollebeek, 2016). The above studies demonstrate the richness of co-branding studies.

Further, evidence suggests that the positive effects of cobranding are prominent under certain conditions. For example, consumers' involvement with the alliance is greater when pre-alliance involvement with the individual partner brands is high (Mazodier & Merunka, 2014). Wang et al. (2020) show that self-congruity, that is, the perceived fit between the brand and the consumer's actual and ideal selves also positively influences the evaluation of the co-brand. The above authors also take into account the dialectical self, which is the degree of cognitive tendency to tolerate the inconsistencies in one's self-concept. Although the above studies demonstrate a substantive body of empirical evidence, further research could focus on marketing-related factors, such as price premium, retailer influence, advertising recency and frequency, alliances between social media influencers and brands, consumer resistance to innovations, and risk thresholds. Such studies could shed further light on this expanding and practitioner popular subject.

6.3 Spill Over Effects in Co-branding

Research in co-branding is an offshoot of brand extension studies, wherein several studies have established the phenomenon of image 'spillover' (e.g., Aaker & Keller, 1990; Ahluwalia et al., 2001; Balachander & Ghose, 2003; Keller & Aaker, 1992). The associations or perceptions towards a brand are carried forward when consumers are asked to evaluate the brand extension. The effect has been applied and tested in co-branding in a number of studies (e.g., Newmeyer et al., 2014; Park et al., 1996; Radighieri et al., 2014; Raufeisen et al., 2019; Simonin & Ruth, 1998). In a brand alliance, the premise of spill over effects is that the *partner* brands are presented in context of another brand, so that judgements about the brand alliance are likely to be affected by prior attitudes towards each individual brand, and subsequent judgements about each brand are likely to be affected by the context of the other brand. Simonin and Ruth (1998) suggest that an alliance represents new evaluations and associations for both brands, therefore attitudes towards each participating brand can alter evaluations when consumers process information about the partnership. Spillover effects therefore reflect changes in consumers' brand evaluations, before and after exposure to new information concerning an alliance. Studies show that spillover effects can be positive or negative. Positive spillover effects occur when brand associations strengthen or enhance a consumer's subsequent attitude or evaluation of the partner brands or the alliance (e.g., Newmeyer et al., 2014; Washburn et al., 2004). When the evaluation of partner brands and of the alliance is adversely affected following exposure to new information, there is evidence of negative spillover effects (e.g., Thomas & Fowler, 2016; Votolato & Unnava, 2006).

Extant literature has shown that perceptions towards the brand alliance is an important factor in determining the likelihood of positive spillover effects on one or both partner brands (e.g., Raufeisen et al., 2019; Rodrigue & Biswas, 2004; Singh, 2016). In this regard, Dickinson and Barker (2007) show that post-alliance attitudes towards the individual partner brands are positively related to the attitudes towards the alliance as a whole. The same effect can be found when positioning perceptions (Singh et al., 2014) and CSR perceptions (Singh, 2016), instead of brand attitudes, are considered. The above studies show that consumers' evaluations of each partner brand impact evaluations of both the alliance and the individual partner brands. Overall, research indicates that attention is mostly directed towards understanding the conditions in which positive spillover from one brand to another occurs. By contrast, research on the conditions and outcomes of negative spillover is sparse. Interestingly. Leuthesser et al. (2003) estimate that as many as 90 percent of alliances are unsuccessful. For example, the alliance between AT&T and British Telecommunications failed in less than two years, amidst losses and incompatible brand vision. Other examples include failures by established brands such as Suzuki and Volkswagen and Hertz and Ryanair. These cases demonstrate that, despite the empirical evidence demonstrating the benefits of the marketing strategy, challenges and difficulties are prevalent in co-branding.

A stream of work concerning negative spillover effect focuses on celebrity endorsement type alliances. For instance, Till and Shimp (1998) show that, given the strong associative link between a celebrity endorser and a brand, negative information about the celebrity has a negative spillover effect and damages the partner brand's reputation. Celebrities frequently experience adverse publicity, and consumers' negative evaluations transfer over to the partner brand. The authors demonstrate that negative information has a greater effect on new or unfamiliar brands for which the association set is relatively scant, than on familiar, established brands where consumers find reasons to reject negative information. In practice, consumers' pre-existing associations towards partners in an alliance are especially insightful for understanding negative spillover effects. In this regard, attribution theory suggests that attributions are more likely to be made for negative events (Folkes, 1988; Weiner, 1985). Consistent with the negativity bias, consumers tend to assign more weight to negative information instead of positive information when forming judgements. In this sense, negative information is highly diagnostic, and as such, very likely to influence judgments (e.g., Ahluwalia, 2002; Herr et al., 1991; Koschate-Fischer et al., 2019; Roehm & Tybout, 2006). In this regard, Votolato and Unnava (2006) demonstrate that negative spillover from a celebrity spokesperson to the brand is likely to occur if the brand is considered to be culpable for the offence. If the brand is directly linked to the negative act, consumers transfer the negative associations concerning the celebrity to the brand. The findings confirm spillover effects and that a non-culpable partner is still vulnerable to crises surrounding the ally if consumers believe that the partner condoned the ally's actions. The authors also demonstrate that the type of negative information that consumers are exposed to can influence post-crisis evaluations and consequently the outcome of negative spillover effects. In another study, Thomas and Fowler (2016) observe that negative spillover effect is reciprocal, that is, brand transgressions influence consumers' attitudes towards the endorsing celebrity, just like celebrity transgressions influence attitudes towards the brand. The authors report that consumers' attitudes towards a celebrity endorser are negative when the brand commits a transgression due to perceptions of co-responsibility that ultimately undermine the moral reputation of the endorser.

In recent advancements, research has demonstrated that when an alliance undergoes a crisis, consumers form negative attitudes towards the allied brand deemed responsible as well as the alliance as a whole (Quamina & Singh, 2019; Turan, 2022). The negative impact of crises therefore transfers to the alliance, thus including the non-culpable partner brand (Singh et al. 2020b). Such an effect appears to vary across crisis types, with preventable crises leading to more negative responses of consumers when compared with accidental ones. For example, the same research demonstrates that, following a preventable crisis, the non-culpable brand in the alliance suffers from negative consumer perceptions even when enjoying high equity (Singh et al., 2020b).

Another notable work on brand crises shows that the brand's response to a crisis can revert the trend by influencing consumer perceptions positively (Singh et al., 2020a). Future studies could explicitly address a comparison between crises affecting an alliance with two corporate brands and those undermining an alliance between a corporate brand and a celebrity. Given the popularity of the social media influencers endorsing brands, further studies in the domain are merited (e.g., Singh et al., 2020c).

6.4 Research on Different Types of Brand Alliances

Although the variety of co-branding arrangements point to the scholarly richness of the domain, the dissimilarities in the nature of the alliances often raise questions about the generalisability of results, as well as the coherence of evidence in the existing body of knowledge. The extant literature refers to different types of co-branding alliances (for a typology see Newmeyer et al., 2018). For instance, an Advertising Alliance is a strategy wherein brands feature together in the same advertisement (Samu et al., 1999). Nguyen et al. (2018) examine whether having two brands in an advertisement is beneficial for both brands. Remarkably, the study finds that advertising two brands has no effect on ad memorability, and has a negative impact on brand recall. In another study on co-branding communications, Roosens et al. (2019) find that the spillover effects from one ally to the other are stronger with explicit brand mentions than with a mere partnership mention. Further, the study shows that there is no added value in two allies communicating jointly, provided that both partners explicitly mention their partner brand. However, when the partner brands communicate separately, reciprocation of an explicit brand mention leads to positive evaluations. Given the importance of return on advertising investment, future studies on advertising alliances can inform how to plan advertising expenditure, in addition to advancing the co-branding literature.

In dual branding alliances, a national brand can produce goods for a retail brand (Cascio et al., 2022; Sethuraman, 2009). The main aim of this co-branding strategy is to increase consumer choice and store loyalty. However, the dynamics and competition between the national brands and the store brands have been the focus of scholars who continue to call for further insights on how store brand strategy contributes to firm success (e.g., Arnett et al., 2010; Bauner et al., 2019; Cascio et al., 2022; Kumar et al., 2017). Dual branding also applies to partnerships between a celebrity endorser and a corporate brand (e.g., Ilicic & Webster, 2013; Seno & Lukas, 2007). In this domain, Tian et al.

(2021) establish the transfer of celebrity traits to brands demonstrating that the changes in brand belief and attitude are consistent with the celebrity's traits. The meaning transfer effect becomes stronger when lesser-known brands are associated with celebrities via co-branding.

The study of social purpose driven branding is well-established in both consumer and industrial marketing. The co-branding strategy known as cause–brand alliance is a partnership between a corporate brand and a social cause (Lafferty et al., 2004). Studies demonstrate positive evaluations concerning both the brand and the social cause as a result of cause-brand alliances (e.g., Alcaniz et al., 2010; Lafferty et al., 2004, Lafferty & Goldsmith, 2005; Sénéchal et al., 2014). In this domain, the study by Alcaniz et al. (2010) shows that image fit and altruistic attribution are cues that consumers employ to evaluate company trustworthiness when the brand is linked to a social cause. Examining alliances between a brand and fair-trade labelling organisation, Sénéchal et al. (2014) show that the corporate brand provides the alliance with a leading position, while the FairTrade brand provides the ethical attribute, thereby making the co-branding strategy beneficial to both parties. Through the lens of balance theory, Yun et al. (2019) show that consumers' attitudes towards a brand and attitudes towards a cause predict perceptions of cause marketing compatibility. The authors also find that cause marketing triadic balance can be predicted when attitude strength is included in the model and there is evidence of attitude spillover effects.

Further research on cause–brand alliances could focus on motive attributions, that is, whether the brand's partnership with a social cause alludes to the ethicality of the brand thus can lower consumer scepticism. Future research could investigate the effectiveness of partnerships between inherently 'stigmatised' brands, such as brands in the fast food or oil industries, and social causes. Research into fit between the social cause and the brand could generate findings that encourage more corporate brands to invest in social causes. Future research could also account for the impact of short-term versus long-term alliances between brands and other entities.

6.5 Brand Partnerships in Business-to-Business Markets

Scholarly research in branding has focused mainly on alliances in business-to-consumers settings. Over the past decade or so, however, there has been growing impetus on Business-to-Business (B2B) research and scholars concur that branding plays an important role in industrial markets as well (e.g., Leek & Christodoulides, 2011; Österle et al., 2018; Sheth & Sinha, 2015). Despite the advances, the literature on partnerships in B2B settings is still sparse, except for a handful of studies (e.g., Bengtsson & Servais, 2005; Crisafulli et al., 2020; Kalafatis et al., 2014). In an early study, Bucklin and Sengupta (1993) suggest that, in industrial branding, the buying process involves complex purchases, and branding plays an important role towards reducing risk and uncertainty. The study notes that co-branding in B2B markets is a viable strategy, and helps the partners to gain managerial resources, credibility, and trust. In another study, Dahlstrom and Dato-on (2004) examine the viable evaluation criteria for forming partnerships in the retail distribution sector. In particular, research in the domain addresses knowledge of buyers (Norris, 1993), market differentiation (Ghosh & John, 2009), the benefits of B2B branding in increased stock returns (Cao & Yan, 2017), along with the drawbacks of alliances, such as role stress and conflict (Dahlstrom & Nygaard, 2016). Other studies have examined ingredient branding in the B2B context, showing that ingredient service brands impact buyer preferences in B2B markets (e.g., Erevelles et al., 2008; Helm & Özergin, 2015). Overall, the above studies have advanced knowledge on the viability of B2B brand alliances.

Another stream of studies on B2B co-branding uses methodological approaches that are novel to B2B research. For example, employing experimental design, Kalafatis et al. (2012) have examined the impact of partner brand characteristics such as brand equity. The authors show that brands with equivalent equity levels share the benefits of the co-branding equally, yet lower equity brands tend to benefit even more when compared with their higher equity partners. The results suggest that dominant partners gain a greater proportion of functional benefits (such as technical expertise) from the co-branding strategy. In another experimental study, Kalafatis et al. (2014) show the process of evaluation perceptions formation in B2B brand alliances as the result of an assimilation and contrast effect. The above studies have created a novel stream of work based on experimental methods, showing the potential for robust causal B2B research in the future.

The above review of key B2B work however presents a gap in the study of the *purpose* of a B2B alliance, as well as how such a purpose is communicated to existing and potential organisational buyers. In this regard, Berger et al. (2015) in their qualitative study addressing social alliance between a for-profit B2B brand and a non-profit, note the relevance of fit and structural characteristics. The ideas in the above study have been further refined and empirically tested in an experimental work by Crisafulli et al. (2020). The authors show that alliances between non-profits or for-profits aimed at launching social innovations lead to greater purchase intentions of organisational buyers than independent ventures of for-profits. This is due to stereotypes of warmth and competence attributed to the allied partners. Further, the same study demonstrates that communicating societal benefits accruing from a social innovation favours the alliance.

Given the increasing relevance of sustainable and social purpose driven branding, future studies should extend the above work. For instance, research could examine the model for-profits and non-profits whose mission partially fits or does not fit with the social innovation purpose. A future study could test how the established brand attributes such as equity, knowledge, familiarity, and trust influence the success of social alliances in B2B markets. Another fruitful area of research is the alliance between a B2B brand and an influencer or an opinion leader (e.g., see Crisafulli et al., 2022).

References

Aaker, D. A. & Keller, K. L. (1990). Consumer evaluations of brand extensions. *Journal of Marketing*, *54*(1), 27–41.

Abratt, R. & Motlana, P. (2000). Managing cobranding strategies: Global brands into local markets. *Business Horizons*, *45*(5), 43–50.

Ahluwalia, R. (2002). How prevalent is the negativity effect in consumer environments? *Journal of Consumer Research*, 29, 270–279.

Ahluwalia, R., Unnava, H. R., & Burnkrankt, R. E. (2001). The moderating role of commitment on the spillover effect of marketing communications. *Journal of Marketing Research*, *38*(4), 458–470.

Ahn, J., Kim, A., & Sung, Y. (2020). The effects of sensory fit on consumer evaluations of co-branding. *International Journal of Advertising*, *39*(4), 486–503.

Alcañiz, E. B., Cáceres, R. C., & Pérez, R. C. (2010). Alliances between brands and social causes: The influence of company credibility on social responsibility image. *Journal of Business Ethics*, *96*(2), 169–186.

Arnett, D. B., Laverie, D. A., & Wilcox, J. B. (2010). A longitudinal examination of the effects of retailer-manufacturer brand alliances: The role of perceived fit. *Journal of Marketing Management*, *26*(2), 5–27.

Balachander, S. & Ghose, S. (2003). Reciprocal spill over effects: A strategic benefit of brand extension. *Journal of Marketing*, *67*(1), 4–13.

Baumgarth, C. (2004). Evaluations of co-brands and spill-over effects: Further empirical results. *Journal of Marketing Communications*, *10*(2), 115–131.

Bauner, C., Jaenicke, E., Wang, E., & Wu, P.-C. (2019). Couponing strategies in competition between a national brand and a private label product. *Journal of Retailing*, *95*(1), 57–66.

Bengtsson, A., & Servais, P. (2005). Co-branding on industrial markets. *Industrial Marketing Management, 34*(7), 706–713.

Berger, I. E., Cunningham, P. H., & Drumwright, M. E. (2015). Social alliances: Company/nonprofit collaboration. *California Management Review, 47*(1), 58–90.

Besharat, A. (2010). How co-branding versus brand extensions drive consumers' evaluations of new products: A brand equity approach. *Industrial Marketing Management, 39*(8), 1240–1249.

Besharat, A., & Langan, R. (2014). Towards the formation of consensus in the domain of co-branding: Current findings and future priorities. *Journal of Brand Management, 21*(2), 112–132.

Bouten, L. M., Snelders, D., & Hultink, E. J. (2011). The impact of fit measures on the consumer evaluation of new co-branded products. *Journal of Product Innovation Management, 28*(4), 455–469.

Bucklin, L. P., & Sengupta, S. (1993). Organising successful co-marketing alliances. *Journal of Marketing, 57*(2), 32–46.

Cao, Z., & Yan, R. (2017). Does brand partnership create a happy marriage? The role of brand value on brand alliance outcomes of partners. *Industrial Marketing Management, 67*, 148–157.

Cascio, A., Waites, S. F., Moore, R., Moore, M., Vorhies, D. W., & Bentley, J. P. (2022). The effects of dual branding rumors on consumers' national and store brand evaluations. *Journal of Marketing Theory and Practice*, 1–18.

Chaudhuri, A., & Holbrook, M. B. (2001). The chain of effects from brand trust and brand effect to brand performance: The role of brand loyalty. *Journal of Marketing, 65*(4), 81–93.

Crisafulli, B., Dimitriu, R., & Singh, J. (2020). Joining hands for the greater good: Examining social innovation launch strategies in B2B settings. *Industrial Marketing Management, 89*, 487–498.

Crisafulli, B., Quamina, L., & Singh, J. (2022). Competence is power: How digital influencers impact buying decisions in B2B markets. *Industrial Marketing Management, 104*, 384–399.

Dahlstrom, R., & Dato-on, M. C. (2004). Business-to-business antecedents to retail co-branding. *Journal of Business-to-Business Marketing, 11*(3), 1–22.

Dahlstrom, R., & Nygaard, A. (2016). The psychology of co-branding alliances: The business-to-business relationship outcomes of role stress. *Psychology & Marketing, 33*(4), 267–282.

Das, T. K., & Teng, B. S. (1998). Between trust and control: Developing confidence in partner cooperation in alliances. *Academy of Management Review, 23*(3), 491–512.

Desai, K. K., & Keller, K. L. (2002). The effects of ingredient branding strategies on host brand extendibility. *Journal of Marketing, 66*, 73–93.

Dickinson, S., & Barker, A. (2007). Evaluations of branding alliances between non-profit and commercial brand partners: The transfer of affect. *International Journal of Nonprofit and Voluntary Sector Marketing, 12*(1), 75–89.

Dutta, S., & Pullig, C. (2011). Effectiveness of corporate responses to brand crises: The role of crisis type and response strategies. *Journal of Business Research, 64*(12), 1281–1287.

Erevelles, S., Stevenson, T. H., Srinivasan, S., & Fukawa, N. (2008). An analysis of B2B ingredient co-branding relationships. *Industrial Marketing Management, 37*(8), 940–952.

Folkes, V. S. (1988). Recent attribution research in consumer behavior: A review and new directions. *Journal of Consumer Research, 14*(4), 548–565.

Fullerton, G. (2003). When does commitment lead to loyalty? *Journal of Service Research, 5*(4), 333–344.

Ghosh, M., & John, G. (2009). When should original equipment manufacturers use branded component contracts with suppliers? *Journal of Marketing Research, 46*(5), 597–611.

Helm, S. V. & Ozergin, B. (2015). Service inside: The impact of ingredient service branding on quality perceptions and behavioral intentions. *Industrial Marketing Management, 50*, 142–149 October.

Helmig, B., Huber, J. A., & Leeflang, P. (2007). Explaining behavioural intentions toward co-branded products. *Journal of Marketing Management, 23*(3–4), 285–304.

Helmig, B., Huber, J. A., & Leeflang, P. S. (2008). Co-branding: The state of the art. *Schmalenbach Business Review, 60*(4), 359–377.

Herr, P. M., Kardes, F. R., & Kim, J. (1991). Effects of word-of-mouth and product-attribute information of persuasion: An accessibility-diagnosticity perspective. *Journal of Consumer Research, 17*, 454–462.

Ilicic, J. & Webster, C. M. (2013). Celebrity co-branding partners as irrelevant brand information in advertisements. *Journal of Business Research, 66*(7), 941–947.

Kalafatis, S. P., Ledden, L., Riley, D., & Singh, J. (2016). The added value of brand alliances in higher education. *Journal of Business Research, 69*(8), 3122–3132.

Kalafatis, S. P., Remizova, N., Riley, D., & Singh, J. (2012). The differential impact of brand equity on B2B co-branding. *The Journal of Business and Industrial Marketing, 27*(8), 623–634.

Kalafatis, S. P., Riley, D., & Singh, J. (2014). Context effects in the evaluation of business-to-business brand alliances. *Industrial Marketing Management, 43*(2), 322–334.

Keller, K. L., & Aaker, D. A. (1992). The effects of sequential introduction of brand extensions. *Journal of Marketing Research, 29*(1), 35–50.

Koschate-Fischer, N., Hoyer, W., & Wolframm, C. (2019). What if something unexpected happens to my brand? Spillover effects from positive and negative events in a co-branding partnership. *Psychology and Marketing, 36*(8), 758–772.

Kumar, V., Anand, A., & Song, H. (2017). Future of retailer profitability: An organizing framework. *Journal of Retailing, 93*(1), 96–119.

Lafferty, B. A., & Goldsmith, R. E. (2005). Cause–brand alliances: Does the cause help the brand or does the brand help the cause? *Journal of Business Research, 58*(4), 423–429.

Lafferty, B. A., Goldsmith, R. E., & Hult, G. (2004). The impact of the alliance on the partners: A look at cause-brand alliances. *Psychology and Marketing, 21*(7), 509–531.

Lambe, C. J., Spekman, R. E., & Hunt, S. D. (2002). Alliance competence, resources, and alliance success: Conceptualization, measurement, and initial test. *Journal of the Academy of Marketing Science, 30*(2), 141–158.

Lebar, E., Buehler, P., Keller, K. L., Sawicka, M., Aksehirli, Z., & Richey, K. (2005). Brand equity implications of joint branding programs. *Journal of Advertising Research, 45*(4), 413–425.

Leek, S., & Christodoulides, G. (2011). A literature review and future agenda for B2B branding: Challenges of branding in a B2B context. *Industrial Marketing Management, 40*(6), 830–837.

Leuthesser, L., Kohli, C., & Suri, R. (2003). 2+2= 5? A framework for using co-branding to leverage a brand. *Journal of Brand Management, 11*(1), 35–47.

Mazodier, M. & Merunka, D. (2014). Beyond brand attitude: Individual drivers of purchase for symbolic cobranded products. *Journal of Business Research. 67*(7), 1552–1558.

Moon, H. & Sprott, D. E. (2016). Ingredient branding for a luxury brand: The role of brand and product fit. *Journal of Business Research, 69*(12), 5768–5774.

Naidoo, V. & Hollebeek, L. D. (2016). Higher education brand alliances: Investigating consumers' dual-degree purchase intentions. *Journal of Business Research, 69*(8), 3113–3121.

Newmeyer, C. E., Venkatesh, R., & Chatterjee, R. (2014). Cobranding arrangements and partner selection: A conceptual framework and managerial guidelines. *Journal of the Academy of Marketing Science, 42*(2), 103–118.

Newmeyer, C. E., Venkatesh, R., Ruth, J. A. & Chatterjee, R. (2018). A typology of brand alliances and consumer awareness of brand alliance integration. *Marketing Letters, 29*(3), 275–289.

Nguyen, C., Romaniuk, J., Faulkner, M. & Cohen, J. (2018). Are two brands better than one? Investigating the effects of co-branding in advertising on audience memory. *Marketing Letters, 29*(1), 37–48.

Norris, D. G. (1993). Intel inside: Branding a component in a business market. *Journal of Business and Industrial Marketing, 8*(1), 14–24.

Österle, B., Kuhn, M. M., & Henseler, J. (2018). Brand worlds: Introducing experiential marketing to B2B branding. *Industrial Marketing Management, 72*, 71–98.

Park, C, Jun, S., & Shocker, A. (1996). Composite branding alliances: An investigation of extension and feedback effects. *Journal of Marketing Research, 33*(4), 453–466.

Pinello, C., Picone, P. M., & Mocciaro Li Destri, A. (2022). Co-branding research: Where we are and where we could go from here. *European Journal of Marketing*, 56(2), 584–621.

Quamina, L. & Singh, J. (2019). Negative spill over effects in corporate brand alliances in crisis. *American Marketing Association Winter Conference*, Austin, TX, USA.

Radighieri, J. P., Mariadoss, B. J., Grégoire, Y. & Johnson, J. L. (2014). Ingredient branding and feedback effects: The impact of product outcomes, initial parent brand strength asymmetry, and parent Brand role. *Marketing Letters*, 25(2), 123–138.

Rao, A. R., Qu, L., & Ruekert, R. W. (1999). Signaling unobservable product quality through a brand ally. *Journal of Marketing Research*, 36(2), 258–268.

Raufeisen, X., Wulf, L., Köcher, S., Faupel, U., & Holzmüller, H. H. (2019). Spillover effects in marketing: Integrating core research domains. *AMS Review*, 9(3), 249–267.

Rodrigue, C. S. & Biswas, A. (2004). Brand alliance dependency and exclusivity: An empirical investigation. *Journal of Product & Brand Management*, 13(7), 477–487.

Roehm, M. L. & Tybout, A. M. (2006). When will a brand scandal spill over, and how should competitors respond? *Journal of Marketing Research*, 43, 366–373.

Roosens, B., Dens, N., & Lievens, A. (2019). Quid pro quo: The impact of explicit brand mentions and reciprocity in brand alliance communications. *European Journal of Marketing*, 53(2), 320–344.

Ruekert, R. W., & Rao, A. (1994). Brand alliances as signals of product quality. *Sloan Management Review*, 36(1), 87–97.

Samu, S., Krishnan, H., & Smith, R. (1999). Using advertising alliances for new product introduction: Interactions between product complementarity and promotional strategies. *Journal of Marketing*, 63(1), 57–74.

Sénéchal, S., Georges, L., & Pernin, J. L. (2014). Alliances between corporate and fair trade brands: Examining the antecedents of overall evaluation of the co-branded product. *Journal of Business Ethics*, 124(3), 365–381.

Seno, D. & Lukas, B. (2007). The equity effect of product endorsement by celebrities: A conceptual framework from a co-branding perspective. *European Journal of Marketing*, 41(1/2), 121–134.

Sethuraman, R. (2009). Assessing the external validity of analytical results from national brand and store brand competition models. *Marketing Science*, 28(4), 759–781.

Sheth, J. N., & Sinha, M. (2015). B2B branding in emerging markets: A sustainability perspective. *Industrial Marketing Management*, 51, 79–88.

Simonin, B. L. & Ruth, J. A. (1998). Is a company known by the company it keeps? Assessing the spillover effects of brand alliances on consumer brand attitudes. *Journal of Marketing Research*, 35(1), 30–42.

Singh, J. (2016). The influence of CSR and ethical self-identity in consumer evaluation of cobrands. *Journal of Business Ethics*, 138(2), 311–326.

Singh, J., Crisafulli, B., & Quamina, L. (2020a). 'Corporate image at stake': The impact of crises and response strategies on consumer perceptions of corporate brand alliances. *Journal of Business Research, 117*, 839–849.

Singh, J., Crisafulli, B., Quamina, L. T., & Kottasz, R. (2020b). The role of brand equity and crisis type on corporate brand alliances in crises. *European Management Review, 17*(4), 821–834.

Singh, J., Crisafulli, B., & Xue, M. T. (2020c). 'To trust or not to trust': The impact of social media influencers on the reputation of corporate brands in crisis. *Journal of Business Research, 119*, 464–480.

Singh, J., Kalafatis, S. P., & Ledden, L. (2014). Consumer perceptions of cobrands: The role of brand positioning strategies. *Marketing Intelligence and Planning, 32*(2), 145–159.

Swaminathan, V., Reddy, S. K., & Dommer, S. L. (2012). Spillover effects of ingredient branded strategies on brand choice: A field study. *Marketing Letters, 23*(1), 237–251.

Tasci, A. D., & Guillet, B. D. (2011). It affects, it affects not: A quasi-experiment on the transfer effect of co-branding on consumer-based brand equity of hospitality products. *International Journal of Hospitality Management, 30*(4), 774–782.

Thomas, V. L. & Fowler, K. (2016). Examining the impact of brand transgressions on consumers' perceptions of celebrity endorsers. *Journal of Advertising, 45*(4), 377–390.

Tian, S., Tao, W., Hong, C., & Tsai, W. H. S. (2021). Meaning transfer in celebrity endorsement and co-branding: Meaning valence, association type, and brand awareness. *International Journal of Advertising, 6*, 1–21.

Till, B. D., & Shimp, T. A. (1998). Endorsers in advertising: The case of negative celebrity information. *Journal of Advertising, 27*(1), 67–82.

Turan, C. P. (2021). Success drivers of co-branding: A meta-analysis. *International Journal of Consumer Studies, 45*(4), 911–936.

Turan, C. P. (2022). Deal or deny: The effectiveness of crisis response strategies on brand equity of the focal brand in co-branding. *Journal of Business Research, 149*, 615–629.

Vaidyanathan, R., & Aggarwal, P. (2000). Strategic brand alliances: Implications of ingredient branding for national and private label brands. *Journal of Product & Brand Management, 9*(4), 214–228.

Votolato, N. L., & Unnava, H. R. (2006). Spillover of negative information on brand alliances. *Journal of Consumer Psychology, 16*(2), 196–202.

Wang, W., Chen, C. H. S., Nguyen, B., & Shukla, P. (2020). Collaboration between East and West: Influence of consumer dialectical self on attitude towards co-brand personality traits. *International Marketing Review, 37*(6), 1155–1180.

Washburn, J. H., Till, B. D. & Priluck, R. (2000). Co-branding: Brand equity and trial effects. *Journal of Consumer Marketing, 17*(7), 591–604.

Washburn, J. H., Till, B. D., & Priluck, R. (2004). Brand alliance and customer-based brand-equity effects. *Psychology & Marketing, 21*(7), 487–508.

Weiner, B. (1985). An attributional theory of achievement motivation and emotion. *Psychological Review, 92*(4), 548.

Yun, J. T., Duff, B. R., Vargas, P., Himelboim, I., & Sundaram, H. (2019). Can we find the right balance in cause-related marketing? Analyzing the boundaries of balance theory in evaluating brand-cause partnerships. *Psychology & Marketing, 36*(11), 989–1002.

7 New Approaches to Brand–Consumer Research

7.1 Introduction

Creating positive brand associations has long been a responsibility of brand management practice. Quantifying and measuring such associations have, however, never been easy tasks for marketing professionals and scholars. Neuroscientific methods are increasingly being recognised as a valuable alternative to traditional approaches to consumer research that can develop explanations about the impact of branding on consumers' cognition, emotion and behaviour. Neuromarketing is a topical area of research in marketing science.

Concurrently, the rapid proliferation of social media presents opportunities and challenges for scholarly research. Brands have novel strategies at their disposal to interact with consumers on social media. Among others, influencer marketing continues to gain prominence in companies' digital marketing strategies (Association of National Advertisers, 2022). Social media offers new types of data to understand brands and consumers. Yet, the noise, volume, and opacity of such data poses challenges in examining brand perceptions (Culotta & Cutler, 2016). Researchers have focused on the development of automated estimation methods that can handle large volume of unstructured, ambiguous data. Furthermore, attention is being directed towards explaining the interface between brands and consumers in emerging and base of the pyramid (BoP) markets, which is a research area long overlooked by branding scholars.

This chapter appraises novel approaches and methods to brand–consumer research. It reviews the latest evidence on how brands employ influencer marketing and how consumers relate to influencers. It also presents state-of-the-art research on neuroscientific methods and branding in BoP markets. The chapter ends with directions for future research in multiple branding domains.

DOI: 10.4324/9780429449598-7

7.2 Brands and Social Media Influencers

With the growth of e-commerce, brands have been focusing on building corporate websites that strengthen brand associations and reinforce a positive brand experience (Christodoulides & de Chernatony, 2004; Simoes et al., 2015). Corporate websites add value if able to communicate brand personality, corporate brand image, and are easy to locate and navigate. With the advent of web 2.0 and social media, the elements mentioned above have become 'hygiene factors' that no longer add value, as contended by Borel and Christodoulides (2016). The presence of such elements, while remaining essential to building brand equity, nowadays does not represent a differentiator. Crucially, user-generated content (UGC) has changed the way brands and consumers communicate, and the weight given to one or the other player. In fact, the way the brand communicates about itself is increasingly less important than how consumers and communities of interest communicate about the brand (Buzeta et al., 2020). Consistent with the value creation perspective advocated by Vargo and Lusch (2004), consumers are progressively proactive contributors to brand interactions, not passive receivers of branded content. A wide range of new functionalities are available, including pod/vodcasts, video sharing, blogs, widgets. Consumers create user-generated content about the brand, upload it on social media platforms for everybody to read and generate engagement that can at times even interfere with the personality characteristics and values conveyed by the brand. On some occasions, the brand itself asks consumers to generate social media content that backfires. A case in point concerns the #McDStories campaign by McDonald's. McDonald's wanted their customers to use the #McDStories hashtag to share their nice experiences with the brand on Twitter. Following some paid tweets about heart-warming stories, McDonald's was reminded by consumers of the brand's failures and shortcomings. Instead of getting coverage about the brand's past good deeds, customer complaints surfaced. Invariably, such stories also gained the attention of the press which further amplified the negative effect. Even brands of social networking sites (SNSs) are nowadays facing highly vocal consumers whose opinions and online content needs to be attended to. Online aggression is, for instance, a recurrent issue on Twitter. In a still largely unregulated environment, Twitter is faced with the dilemma of banning online aggressors or giving them a 'free ride' on the grounds of protecting free speech. Preliminary research evidence in this sphere (e.g., Antonetti & Crisafulli, 2021) indicates that consumers closely scrutinise how brands of SNSs handle online controversies and generally oppose user bans on Twitter, unless a justification for the ban is provided publicly by brands.

Leveraging on the speed of adoption and scalability of social media, some consumers have established a strong online identity, an appeal to a mass audience, and built a follower base, transforming into social media influencers. Often also referred to as social media stars or micro-celebrities, influencers are persuasive online personalities who influence followers' perceptions and behaviour (e.g., Gaenssle & Budzinski, 2020; Kim et al., 2021). Taking the centre stage on various social media platforms such as Instagram, TikTok, YouTube and Facebook, influencers are believed to build credibility and popularity by forging communal relationships based on collaboration and mutual benefits with followers (Cocker & Cronin, 2017). Influencers gain from wide reach, typically measured in terms of the size of the follower base, their influence on the public's decision-making, and the intimate bond they create with followers (Hudders et al., 2021). In light of the above aspects, brands increasingly partner with influencers to promote offerings and reach mass audiences, a practice commonly known as influencer marketing. In some instances, influencers are even employed to bolster the brand's communication in the event of corporate crises as further discussed in Section 7.4. Investment in influencer marketing is estimated to be worth $15 billion by the end of 2022 (Forbes, 2022).

With the popularity of influencers as a marketing tool, scholarly interest has spurred research in the field. Studies have examined the types of influencers on social media, influencers' characteristics, and their impact on followers, with much of the evidence being in support of the role of influencers in endorsing business offerings and driving profit-able business outcomes (for a literature review, see Hudders et al., 2021; Vrontis et al., 2021). Evidence suggests that influencers impact followers' purchase intentions through building parasocial relationships, that is, in the form of make-believe relationships developed by consumers with a media personality (e.g., Farivar et al., 2021). Simultaneously, emerging evidence shows situations that add caveats to the impact of influencer marketing. For instance, Singh et al. (2020a) show that influencers' involvement in brands' communications following crises creates dis-trust about the brand's intent. As a result, consumers report inferences of manipulative intent, which in turn negatively affect perceived trust-worthiness and corporate reputation. Other studies raise concerns about the ethics of influencers' activities, for instance, when promoting the commercial practice of momblogging with caregiving tasks (Archer, 2019), when seeking to remain authentic while providing travel advice (Wellman et al., 2020), and in relation to the online harassment and hate emails suffered by influencers themselves (Novoselova & Jenson,

2019). The emerging evidence therefore exposes the advantages, but also the limitations of brand management practices promoting investment in influencer marketing.

Influencer marketing represents a vibrant area of work where further research is needed. Prior studies mainly focus on the role of influencers in shaping perceptions towards consumer brands. Comparatively fewer studies have addressed influencer marketing in business-to-business settings, wherein managers or a buying centre make complex purchase decisions. In a groundbreaking study in this sphere, Crisafulli et al. (2022) examine how the stereotype traits of influencers shape purchasing managers' intentions to buy influencer-endorsed technological business solutions. Given the rising popularity of the influencers in the B2B domain, further research is merited to add the growing body of knowledge. In addition, extant research is generally supportive of brand–influencer partnerships given followers' desire to mimic influencers (Ki & Kim, 2019) and the downstream positive outcomes for businesses. By contrast, Singh et al. (2020a) propose a more circumspect approach towards influencer marketing. All in all, the theory of influencer marketing is still emerging, and scholarly publications can contribute to further understanding on the mechanisms through which influencer marketing creates opportunities and challenges for brands (Leung et al., 2022).

In advancing knowledge in this field, an important area to consider relates to the ethical implications of influencer marketing practices. Some influencers create their own brand identity, gain status and distinction by displaying aspiring lifestyles online (Eckhardt & Bardhi, 2019). Such a practice has, however, important ethical implications. Influencers' portrayal of an idealised self raises the question of whether the need to maintain legitimacy and mass online influence should come at the cost of compromising ethicality. A current debate, for instance, regards the use of photoshop to obscure physical or appearance-related imperfections of influencers (Dogson, 2020; Verrastro et al., 2020). Images employed on influencers' online profile might activate social comparisons that ultimately affect how followers view themselves and their perceived well-being. Such a trend could be compounded even further by technological advances enabling the development of computer-generated influencers constructed by artificial intelligence (Mrad et al., 2021). Future research could advance knowledge by addressing the above issues.

7.3 Methodological Advances in Consumer–Brand Research

As discussed in Section 7.1, consumers nowadays have a much more active role in shaping brands' image and associations. Consumers talk within their online network about brands, events and products, in what is commonly referred to as UGC. Crucially, social media offer a platform for UGC to propagate quickly and reach wide, geographically spread audiences.

Within such a landscape, there is need to capture vast data generated by UGC. New approaches to analysing such data have emerged. For instance, Twitter data and text mining approaches fully automate the estimation of consumer perceptions of brand attributes (see Culotta & Cutler, 2016 for an illustration). Through mining Twitter data, Rust et al. (2021) have developed a social media-based brand reputation tracker for the world's top 100 brands. It is evident that text, whether in the form of online reviews, Twitter comments or social media posts, has gained currency. New approaches and software to carry out automated text analysis have been developed as a result. An example is the LIWC software (Pennebaker et al., 2015) employed to extract the sentiment from sections of text written by consumers (for an overview of automated text analysis approaches, see Berger et al., 2020). Computerised techniques have also been developed to examine the narrative content of online reviews, that is the extent to which a review tells a story (e.g., van Laer et al., 2019).

Despite the above methodological advances, the newly emerging data continue to pose challenges to the development of analytical approaches. As pointed out by Culotta and Cutler (2016), social media data such as Twitter comments is large in volume, highly ambiguous and involves noise. Additional research can triangulate existing methods and widen understanding of all aspects of brands, their meaning and effects on consumers (Keller, 2021). Furthermore, with consumer-to-consumer interactions being on the rise, it is plausible that capturing perceptions of one consumer group will only be partially insightful. Brand meaning is being influenced – either positively or negatively – by the experiences of unknown others exposing opinions online (Keller, 2021). Developing approaches that can capture the sentiment of multiple stakeholders concurrently could be the next frontline of branding research.

7.4 Neuroscience in Branding

Over the years, numerous new quantitative and qualitative techniques have been introduced to study consumers and markets, as well as consumers and brands (Keller, 2021). The term 'neuromarketing' was coined in 2002 to indicate "the study of the cerebral mechanism to understand consumer behaviour in order to improve marketing strategies" (Lim, 2018, p. 206). Currently, this represents an interdisciplinary field wherein neuroscientific principles and techniques are applied to solving marketing problems.

Amidst a variety of approaches, including innovative approaches to analysing social media data (see discussion in Section 7.2), neural and physiological research into brands and branding has made notable progress over the years (e.g., Chan et al., 2018; Chen et al., 2015; Karmarkar & Plassmann, 2019; Plassmann et al., 2015; Yoon et al., 2006). Neuroscientific methods such as electroencephalography (EEG), steady-state topography, eye tracking, functional magnetic resonance imaging (fMRI), facial electromyography and electrocardiography have been applied to branding research. Neuroscience methods such as fMRI, eye tracking, EEG and other biometrics (i.e., physiological measures used to characterise human behaviour) have also been used by consumer product brands, such as Coca-Cola to evaluate consumer responses to their ads. Likewise, General Electric has launched research centres using EEG methods to study consumer responses to food and taste.

Neuroscientific methods first gained relevance in psychological research wherein scholars aimed to develop a neuropsychologically sound theory of consumer behaviour (see Plassmann et al., 2012 for a review). In this domain, research has established a link between consumers' brain system and brands. There is, for instance, evidence that the brain system consisting of the ventromedial prefrontal cortex (vmPFC) and the dorsolateral prefrontal cortex (dlPFC) encodes behavioural preferences (e.g., Plassmann et al., 2007). Brand familiarity is linked to memory-related neural pathways in the frontal and temporal lobes (Esch et al., 2012; Klucharev et al., 2008), and interactions with luxury brands is associated with strong activations in vmPFC and striatum, which are known for their role in reward processing (McClure et al., 2004; Plassmann et al., 2007; Schaefer & Rotte, 2007). The evidence from neuropsychological research on consumers has informed neuromarketing research. In marketing, neuroscientific methods have been seen as a more robust alternative to self-reported data, likely to generate more objective findings (Dimoka, 2010; Yoon et al., 2009). Objectivity is linked to the ability of neuroscientific methods to capture both unconscious, emotional processes (Kenning & Plassmann, 2008; Yoon et al., 2012), rewards (O'Doherty, 2004), and participants' behaviour following decision-making (Craig et al., 2012; Hedgcock & Rao, 2009). Unlike the brand personality instrument (Aaker, 1997) and qualitative reports based on imagery elicitation (Roth, 1994), free associations (Krishnan, 1996) or concept mapping techniques (John et al., 2006) which seek to translate mental brand associations into words, neuroscientific methods are treated as reliable approaches to capturing both consumer knowledge of brands through activity in specific brain areas and momentary emotional appraisals that cannot be captured by self-reported indicators (Kolar et al., 2021).When compared with five other approaches (traditional self-reports, implicit measures, eye tracking, biometrics, EEG), fMRI has been found to explain the most variance in advertising elasticities (Venkatraman et al., 2015).

Scholarly evidence demonstrates various applications of neuroscientific methods to marketing (see Daugherty & Thomas, 2018 for a special issue on the topic of neuromarketing). By employing fMRI, Rampl et al. (2016) have shown that decision-making for most attractive employer brands is associated with an increased activation of brain areas linked to emotions and with decreased activation of areas linked to working memory and reasoning. Using the same neuroimaging technique, Chan et al. (2018) have been able to develop neural profiles of brand image and their association with consumers' self-report perceptions of brands. Through the use of EEG, which captures brainwave activity by measuring how brain cells (i.e., neurons) communicate with each other (Lin et al., 2018), scholars have been able to capture cognitive processes in the form of attitudes and preferences, as well as affect and emotions. In a study on brand extensions, Ma et al. (2010) have found that consumers' brainwave activity is enhanced when a new clothing brand is presented and emotions are primed. The same authors emphasise the importance of emotions and product category in the evaluation of brand extensions. In another study, Pozharliev et al. (2015) have employed EEG to demonstrate that the late positive potential, namely a component over visual cortical areas reflecting emotional processes, is enhanced when consumers purchase luxury brands, and even more so when other consumers observe the purchase.

Despite the above advances, research in neuromarketing is still relatively new (Lim, 2018). There are a number of avenues for further research. For instance, a recent review of the literature on consumer emotions in innovation adoption suggests that emotions are important, unfold over time as consumers evaluate, trial, adopt and habitually use innovations such as new brands (Valor et al., 2022). Future studies in neuromarketing could advance research by applying neuroscientific methods that measure the intensity and valence of anticipated and/or experienced emotions concerning a brand, with the view of explicating how emotions unfold across the stages of new brand adoption. In this regard, recent evidence in advertising research suggests that, when compared with surveys, EEG is a superior technique in capturing unconscious appraisal of emotions and visual attention (Kolar et al., 2021).

Further, research on consumers and brands has traditionally captured intentional outcomes. Neuroscientific methods could be leveraged to comprehend behavioural marketing outcomes. Neuromarketing scholars could investigate actual purchase choice and post-purchase recommendations, along with implicit cognitive processes such as assessing benefits and costs, and emotional processes, such as impulsiveness (Lim, 2018).

The area of neuromarketing is, however, not short of criticisms. Ethics is, to date, a highly sensitive issue with regards to the application of neuroscientific techniques to marketing (Pop et al., 2014). The ethical dilemma particularly concerns two aspects of neuromarketing research, namely the vulnerability of participants and the scientific reliability and transparency of methods. Despite following ethical procedures to conducting research, neuroscientific methods could pose a threat to the autonomy of participants, especially the vulnerable (Lim, 2018). Such an ethical concern is even more prominent if neuroscience research is conducted for commercial purposes. Likewise, the implementation of neuroscientific approaches and the interpretation of findings requires high levels of neuroscientific expertise. Lack of such expertise in the wider academic community could hinder the ability to replicate studies and to accurately report reliable findings while also leading to the overestimation of findings (Plassmann et al., 2012; Poldrack, 2006). In light of the above, methodological papers elucidating best practices in conducting and reviewing neuromarketing research could make valuable contributions to the domain.

7.5 Branding in the Event of Crises

There is wide recognition among marketing scholars and practitioners that a brand with high equity plays a strategic role in the success of the organisation. A brand acts as a signal of quality, thereby reassuring consumers of the value of the product or service at the time of purchase (Rao et al., 1999). Likewise, dominant brands, which also tend to be high in equity, are perceived as attractive by shareholders when making investment decisions, and by job seekers looking for employment (Highhouse et al., 2007; Lievens & Slaughter, 2016). Dominance of brands signals that the company is prestigious (Highhouse et al., 2009), and offers attractive compensation and opportunities for career progression (Lievens & Highhouse, 2003). For the organisation, a successful brand can also enhance image among existing employees. Notwithstanding, all too often brands fail to deliver upon the very same values that internal and external stakeholders care about. Cases of brand transgressions, wherein a brand demonstrates disregard for important norms endorsed by consumers, are recurrent and put the integrity of organisations into question (Aaker et al., 2004). Relatedly, brands at times experience product-harm crises wherein products are defective and dangerous to customers (e.g., Cleeren et al., 2017), or service failures whereby the service performance falls below customer expectations (e.g., Smith et al., 1999). The three types of crises described above represent pivotal 'moments of truth' for brands in their efforts to develop and sustain profitable relationships with consumers (Khamitov et al., 2020).

There is a wealth of research in the service, branding and product-harm domains pertaining to the role of crises in shaping consumer behaviour. Research on brand transgressions shows that events of corporate social irresponsibility undermine the perceived ethicality of the organisation (Antonetti & Anesa, 2017; Shea & Hawn, 2019), and lead to retaliation (Antonetti & Maklan, 2016; Grappi et al., 2013). Yet, there are branding cues that offer a buffer against such negative outcomes. For instance, a *brand's dominance* in the marketplace contributes towards attenuating the negative effects of corporate social irresponsibility on talent recruitment (Antonetti et al., 2021b). As shown in the same study, job seekers are lenient in their reactions when social irresponsibility affects a dominant employer. While social irresponsibility conveys the impression of an uncaring organisation (Shea & Hawn, 2019), market dominance signals that the organisation offers more attractive working conditions than the average organisation in the sector (Jones et al., 2014; Lievens & Highhouse, 2003). Likewise, evidence suggests that CSR efforts of brands act as a reservoir of goodwill following product harm crises (Klein & Dawar, 2004), poor product performance (Chernev & Blair, 2015) and events of incompetence of service firms (Antonetti et al., 2021a), protecting the brand from reputational damages. Similarly, brand equity can provide a buffer against the negative impact of service failures (Brady et al., 2008). Brand equity also matters as a cue in the event of crises affecting brand alliances, where two brands partner to launch a new offering. In such contexts, the equity of the non-culpable partner mitigates the negative effects of accidental (not preventable) crises (Singh et al., 2020b). The above discussion highlights an intriguing dual role of brands – brands can be responsible for crises and yet also the solution to mitigating the potentially detrimental consequences of such negative events.

Beyond the above significant advancements, the literature on brand crises remains vibrant. Several issues warrant further research, as elucidated in a systematic review of the literature on negative events in marketing by Khamitov et al. (2020). As argued by the authors, three types of crises have been analysed in separate streams of literature, namely brand transgressions, service failure and product-harm crises. Knowledge creation efforts would benefit from theoretical perspectives that integrate these three streams of work. Likewise, each literature stream has identified important mediators explicating the cognitive and affective mechanisms by which crises impact various stakeholders. Further research could integrate the identified mediators into a unifying framework, depicting the mechanisms by which negative information about a brand impact key stakeholders.

7.6 Branding in the BoP Markets

There is ample evidence that brands increase the profitability of the organisation (e.g., Aaker, 1996), provide shareholders with confidence in investment decisions and reassure consumers of the quality of offerings (e.g., Kirmani & Rao, 2000). Much of the scholarly evidence on branding has, however, traditionally relied upon data from the developed world (Coffie & Darmoe, 2016). Comparatively less is known about the role of branding in Base of the Pyramid (BoP) markets. These are markets that entail large populations on low income and low purchasing power where multinationals tend to be reluctant to do business (Opoku & Hinson, 2005; Prahalad, 2002, 2004; Prahalad & Hart, 2002). In practice, there is a trend towards 'place branding' practices in African countries, which are classified as among BoP markets (Chikweche & Fletcher, 2011). As pointed out by Wanjiru (2005), branded countries create a positive sense of feeling and familiarity while also inoculating negative associations concerning the state of poverty and degradation associated with the African continent.

With the recognition from businesses that branding can represent a mechanism for creating a competitive advantage for BoP markets such as African countries and organisations, and since the work of Prahalad and Hart (2002), research on BoP markets has gradually evolved (see 2017 special issue on the topic in *Marketing Theory*). Although individuals have low income, such markets are believed to *cumulatively* constitute a strong economic force (Prahalad, 2002; 2012). Naturally, multinationals increasingly find such markets attractive, showing the need for greater business focus on BoP markets. As demonstrated in a systematic review of the literature in the domain (see Dembek et al., 2020), studies examining businesses in the BoP markets span across several fields of work, including strategy, marketing, supply chain and operations management, and innovation. In marketing, more specifically, Garrette and Karnani (2010) demonstrate through case study analysis that multinational firms investing in the marketing of socially useful products – clean water, eyeglasses, and nutritious yoghurt – to BoP markets do not succeed commercially. However, the same study identified profitable ventures in the categories of mobile phones and detergents. The same authors therefore encourage to reflect on the business performance implications of branding in BoP markets. Further, London and Hart (2011) contend that, while living in a globalised world, multiple social–political–economic worlds are invariably affected by marketing efforts. In this sense, BoP markets simply cannot be overlooked in business practice.

Some scholars highlight the ethical implications of marketing practice in BoP markets. For instance, Yurdakul et al. (2017) use qualitative insights from BoP communities in Turkey to propose a reconceptualisation of poverty that includes consumers who feel socially excluded, yet without being at the starvation point. The same authors point to the effect of branding in fostering consumption of certain products that meet consumers' desire for social conformity. Crucially, for consumers in BoP markets, the inability to fulfil desire for social conformity results in social exclusion. In this sense, the global consumer culture acts as a catalyst in nurturing social exclusion. Such a finding highlights to the business outcomes of branding in BoP, and yet equally, to the social responsibility of brands towards minimising social exclusion.

Notwithstanding the above advances in marketing domain, branding research in BoP markets is still limited and only sporadically published in top-ranking journals. Future studies could examine how branding can overcome stereotypes of corruption, poverty, poor governance, often associated with countries at the BoP. Such stereotypes often hinder the opportunities to create a positive image for the markets as a whole, for individual countries as well as organisations (Anholt, 2003, 2005; Chikweche & Fletcher, 2011). In a similar vein, service marketing scholars (e.g., Martin & Hill, 2015) have called for research on how service brands can support populations around the world that live at BoP (see extended discussion in Chapter 4 of this book). Although the profit per customer might be lower, BoP markets are *cumulatively* strong. Hence, profitability can still be large from targeting such markets (Rust, 2020).

References

Aaker, D. A. (1996). Measuring brand equity across products and markets. *California Management Review, 38*(3) 103.

Aaker, J. L. (1997). Dimensions of brand personality. *Journal of Marketing Research, 34*(3), 347–357.

Aaker, J. L., Fournier, S., & Brasel, S. A. (2004). When good brands do bad. *Journal of Consumer Research, 31*, 1–16.

Anholt, S. (2003). *Brand New Justice: The Upside of Global Branding.* Oxford: Butterworth-Heinemann.

Anholt, S. (2005). *Brand New Justice – How Branding Places and Products Can Help the Developing World*, revised edn. Oxford: Butterworth-Heinemann.

Antonetti, P., & Anesa, M. (2017). Consumer reactions to corporate tax strategies: The role of political ideology. *Journal of Business Research, 74*, 1–10.

Antonetti, P., & Crisafulli, B. (2021). "I will defend your right to free speech, provided I agree with you": How social media users react (or not) to online out-group aggression. *Psychology & Marketing, 38*, 1633–1650.

Antonetti, P., Crisafulli, B., & Maklan, S. (2021a). When doing good will not save us: Revisiting the buffering effect of CSR following service failures. *Psychology & Marketing, 38*, 1608–1627.

Antonetti, P., Crisafulli, B., & Tuncdogan, A. (2021b). "Just look the other way": Job seekers' reactions to the irresponsibility of market-dominant employers. *Journal of Business Ethics, 174*, 403–422.

Antonetti, P., & Maklan, S. (2016). An extended model of moral outrage at corporate social irresponsibility. *Journal of Business Ethics, 135*(3), 429–444.

Archer, C. (2019). Social media influencers, post-feminism and neoliberalism: How mum bloggers' 'playbour' is reshaping public relations. *Public Relations Inquiry, 8*(2), 149–166.

Association of National Advertisers. (2022). Influencer marketing. Available at www.ana.net/content/show/id/baa-influencer-marketing (Accessed on 17 August 2022).

Berger, J., Humphreys, A., Ludwig, S., Moe, W. W., Netzer, O., & Schweidel, D. A. (2020). Uniting the tribes: Using text for marketing insight. *Journal of Marketing, 84*(1), 1–25.

Borel, L. & Christodoulides, C. (2016). Branding and Digital Analytics. In *The Routledge Companion to Contemporary Brand Management* (Chapter 17) Dall'Olmo Riley, F., Singh, J., & Blankson, C. (Eds.). London: Routledge (pp. 255–268).

Brady, M. K., Cronin, Jr., J. L., Fox, G. L., & Roehm, M. L. (2008). Strategies to offset performance failures: The role of brand equity. *Journal of Retailing, 84*(2), 151–164.

Buzeta, C., De Pelsmacker, P., & Dens, N. (2020). Motivations to use different social media types and their impact on consumers' online brand-related activities (COBRAs). *Journal of Interactive Marketing, 52*, 79–98.

Chan, H.-Y., Boksem, M., & Smidts, A. (2018). Neural profiling of brands: Mapping brand image in consumers' brains with visual templates. *Journal of Marketing Research*, August, 55(4), 600–615.

Chen, Y. P., Nelson, L. D., & Hsu, M. (2015). From "where" to "what": Distributed representations of brand associations in the human brain. *Journal of Marketing Research*, *52*(4), 453–466.

Chernev, A., & Blair, S. (2015). Doing well by doing good: The Benevolent Halo of corporate social responsibility. *Journal of Consumer Research*, *41*(6), 1412–1425.

Chikweche, T., & Fletcher, R. (2011). Branding at the base of the pyramid: A Zimbabwean perspective. *Marketing Intelligence and Planning*, *29*(3): 247–263.

Christodoulides, G., & de Chernatony, L. (2004). Dimensionalising on- and offline brands' composite equity. *Journal of Product & Brand Management*, *13*(3), 168–179.

Cleeren, K., M. G. Dekimpe, & H. J. van Heerde (2017). Marketing research on product-harm crises: A review, managerial implications, and an agenda for future research. *Journal of the Academy of Marketing Science*, *45*, 593–615.

Cocker, H. L., & Cronin, J. (2017). Charismatic authority and the YouTuber: Unpacking the new cults of personality. *Marketing Theory*, *17*(4), 455–472.

Coffie, S. & Darmoe, J. (2016). Branding in the Base of the Pyramid: Bases for Country and Organizations in Ghana. In *The Routledge Companion to Contemporary Brand Management* (Chapter 26), Dall'Olmo Riley, F., Singh, J., & Blankson, C. (Eds.). London: Routledge.

Craig, A., Loureiro, Y., Wood, S., & Vendemia, J. (2012). Suspicious minds: Exploring neural processes during exposure to deceptive advertising. *Journal of Marketing Research*, *49*(6), 361–372.

Crisafulli, B., Quamina, L. T., & Singh, J. (2022). Competence is power: How digital influencers impact buying decisions in B2B markets. *Industrial Marketing Management*, *104*, 384–399.

Culotta, A., & Cutler, J. (2016). Mining brand perceptions from twitter social networks. *Marketing Science*, *35*(3), 341–537.

Daugherty, T., & Thomas, A. R. (2018). Special issue on neuromarketing. *European Journal of Marketing*, *52*(1/2), 2–3.

Dembek, K., Sivasubramaniam, N., & Chmielewski, D. A. (2020). A systematic review of the bottom/base of the pyramid literature: Cumulative evidence and future directions. *Journal of Business Ethics*, *165*, 365–382.

Dimoka, A. (2010). What does the brain tell us about trust and distrust? Evidence from a functional neuroimaging study. *Management Information Systems Quarterly*, *34*(2), 373–396.

Dogson, L. (2020). I asked influencers to edit my selfies and turn me into an entirely different person, and it just reminded me how damaging it is to chase an unattainable idea of perfection. Available at www.insider.com/infl uencers-edited-my-photos-to-make-me-look-completely-different-2020-6 (Accessed 25 October 2022).

Eckhardt, G. M., & Bardhi, F. (2019). New dynamics of social status and distinction. *Marketing Theory*, *20*(1), 85–102.

Esch, F.-R., Moell, T., Schmitt, B., Elger, C. E.t, Neuhaus, C., & Weber, B. (2012). Brands on the brain: Do consumers use declarative information or experienced emotions to evaluate brands? *Journal of Consumer Psychology*, *22*(1), 75–85.

Farivar, S., Wang, F., & Yuan, Y. (2021). Opinion leadership vs. Para-social relationship: Key factors in influencer marketing. *Journal of Retailing and Consumer Services*, *59*, Article 102371.

Forbes (January, 2022). The state of influencer marketing: Top insights for 2022. Available at www.forbes.com/sites/forbesagencycouncil/2022/01/14/the-state-of-influencer-marketing-top-insights-for-2022/

Gaenssle, S., & Budzinski, O. (2020). Stars in social media: New light through old windows? *Journal of Media Business Studies*, *18*(2), 79–105.

Garrette, B., & Karnani, A. (2010). Challenges in marketing socially useful goods to the poor. *California Management Review*, *52*(4), 29–47.

Grappi, S., Romani, S., & Bagozzi, R. P. (2013). The effects of company off-shoring strategies on consumer responses. *Journal of the Academy of Marketing Science*, *41*(6), 683–704.

Hedgcock, W., & Rao, A. R. (2009). Trade-off aversion as an explanation for the attraction effect: A functional magnetic resonance imaging study. *Journal of Marketing Research*, *46*(1), 1–13.

Highhouse, S., Brooks, M. E., & Gregarus, G. (2009). An organizational impression management perspective on the formation of corporate reputations. *Journal of Management*, *35*(6), 1481–1493.

Highhouse, S., Thornbury, E. E., & Little, I. S. (2007). Social-identity functions of attraction to organizations. *Organizational Behavior and Human Decision Processes*, *103*(1), 134–146.

Hudders, L., De Jans, S., & De Veirman, M. (2021). The commercialization of social media stars: A literature review and conceptual framework on the strategic use of social media influencers. *International Journal of Advertising*, *40*(3), 327–375.

John, D. R., Loken, B., Kim, K., & Monga, A. B. (2006). Brand concept maps: A methodology for identifying brand association networks. *Journal of Marketing Research*, *43*(4), 549–563.

Jones, D. A., Willness, C. R., & Madey, S. (2014). Why are job seekers attracted by corporate social performance? Experimental and field tests of three signal-based mechanisms. *Academy of Management Journal*, *57*(2), 383–404.

Karmarkar, U. R., & Plassmann, H. (2019). Consumer neuroscience: Past, present, and future. *Organizational Research Methods*, *22*(1), 174–195.

Keller, K. L. (2021). The future of brands and branding: An essay on multiplicity, heterogeneity, and integration. *Journal of Consumer Research*, *48*, 527–540.

Kenning, P. H., & Plassmann, H. (2008). How neuroscience can inform consumer research. *IEEE Transactions on Neural Systems and Rehabilitation Engineering*, *16*(6), 532–538.

Khamitov, M., Gregoire, Y., & Suri, A. (2020). A systematic review of brand transgression, service failure recovery and product-harm crisis: Integration and guiding insights. *Journal of the Academy of Marketing Science, 48*, 519–542.

Ki, C.-W., & Kim, Y.-K. (2019). The mechanism by which social media influencers persuade consumers: The role of consumers' desire to mimic. *Psychology & Marketing, 36*(10), 905–922.

Kim, E. A., Duffy, M., & Thorson, E. (2021). Under the influence: Social media influencers' impact on response to corporate reputation advertising. *Journal of Advertising, 50*(2), 119–138.

Kirmani, A., & Rao, A. R. (2000). No pain, no gain: A critical review of the literature on signaling unobservable product quality. *Journal of Marketing, 64*(2), 66–79.

Klein, J., & Dawar, N. (2004). Corporate social responsibility and consumers' attributions and brand evaluations in a product–harm crisis. *International Journal of Research in Marketing, 21*(3), 203–217.

Klucharev, V., Smidts, A., & Fernandez, G. (2008). Brain mechanisms of Persuasion: How 'Expert Power' modulates memory and attitudes," *Social Cognitive and Affective Neuroscience, 3*(4), 353–366.

Kolar, T., Batagelj, Z., Omeragić, I., & Husić-Mehmedović, M. (2021). How moment-to-moment EEG measures enhance ad effectiveness evaluation. *Journal of Advertising Research, 61*(4), 365–381.

Krishnan, H. S. (1996). Characteristics of memory associations: A consumer-based brand equity perspective. *International Journal of Research in Marketing, 13*(4), 389–405.

Leung, F. F., Gu, F. F., & Palmatier, R. W. (2022). Online influencer marketing. *Journal of the Academy of Marketing Science, 50*, 226–251.

Lievens, F., & Highhouse, S. (2003). The relation of instrumental and symbolic attributes to a company's attractiveness as an employer. *Personnel Psychology, 56*(1), 75–102.

Lievens, F., & Slaughter, J. E. (2016). Employer image and employer branding: What we know and what we need to know. *Annual Review of Organizational Psychology and Organizational Behavior, 3*, 407–440.

Lim, W. M. (2018). Demystifying neuromarketing. *Journal of Business Research, 91*, 205–220.

Lin, M.-H., Cross, S. N. N., Jones, W. J., & Childers, T. L. (2018). Applying EEG in consumer neuroscience. *European Journal of Marketing, 52*(1/2), 66–91.

London, T., & Hart, S. (2011). *Next Generation Business Strategies for the Base of the Pyramid: New Approaches for Building Mutual Value*, Upper Saddle River, NJ: FT Press.

Ma, Q., Wang, X., Liangchao, S., & Dai, S. (2010). The influence of negative emotion on brand extension as reflected by the change of N2: A preliminary study. *Neuroscience Letters, 485*(3), 237–240.

Martin, K. D., & Hill, R. P. (2015). Saving and well-being at the base of the pyramid: Implications for transformative financial services delivery. *Journal of Service Research, 18*(3), 405–421.

McClure, S. M., Li, J., Tomlin, D., et al. (2004). Neural correlates of behavioral preference for culturally familiar drinks. *Neuron, 44*(2), 379–387.

Mrad, M., Ramadan, Z., & Nasr, L. I. (2021). Computer-generated influencers: The rise of digital personalities. *Marketing Intelligence & Planning, 40*(5), 589–603.

Novoselova, V., & Jenson, J. (2019). Authorship and professional digital presence in feminist blogs. *Feminist Media Studies, 19*(2), 257–272.

O'Doherty, J. (2004). Reward representations and reward-related learning in the human brain: insights from neuroimaging. *Current Opinion in Neurobiology, 14*(6), 769–776.

Opoku, R., & Hinson, R. (2005). Online brand personalities: An exploratory analysis of selected African countries. *Place Branding, 2*(2), 118–129.

Pennebaker, J. W., Booth, R. J., Boyd, R. L., & Francis, M. E. (2015). *Linguistic Inquiry and Word Count: LIWC2015*. Austin, TX: Pennebaker Conglomerates.

Plassmann, H., Ambler, T., Braeutigam, S., & Kenning, P. (2007). What can advertisers learn from neuroscience? *International Journal of Advertising, 26*(2), 151–175.

Plassmann, H., Ramsøy, T. Z., & Milosavljevic, M. (2012). Branding the brain: A critical review and outlook. *Journal of Consumer Psychology, 22*(1), 18–36.

Plassmann, H., Venkatraman, V., Huettel, S., & Yoon, C. (2015). Consumer neuroscience: Applications, challenges, and possible solutions. *Journal of Marketing Research, 52*(4), 427–435.

Poldrack, R. A. (2006). Can cognitive processes be inferred from neuroimaging data? *Trends in Cognitive Sciences, 10*(2), 59–63.

Pop, N. A., Dabija, D. C., & Iorga, A. M. (2014). Ethical responsibility of neuromarketing companies in harnessing the market research – A global exploratory approach. *Amfiteatru Economic, 16*(35), 26–40.

Pozharliev, R., Verbeke, W. J., Van Strien, J. W., & Bagozzi, R. P. (2015). Merely being with you increases my attention to luxury products: Using EEG to understand consumers' emotional experience with luxury branded products. *Journal of Marketing Research, 52*(4), 546–558.

Prahalad, C. K. (2002). Strategies for the bottom of the economic pyramid: India as a source of innovation. *Society for Organizational Learning Reflections, 3*(4), 6–17.

Prahalad, C. K. (2004). *Fortune at the Bottom of the Pyramid: Eradicating Poverty through Profits,* Upper Saddle River, NJ: Pearson Education.

Prahalad, C. K. (2012). Bottom of the pyramid as a source of breakthrough innovations. *Journal of Product Innovation Management, 29*(1), 6–12.

Prahalad, C. K., & Hart, S. L. (2002). Fortune at the bottom of the pyramid. *Strategy + Business, 29,* 2–14.

Rampl, L.V., Opitz, C., Welpe, I.M. et al. (2016). The role of emotions in decision-making on employer brands: Insights from functional magnetic resonance imaging (fMRI). *Marketing Letters, 27,* 361–374.

Rao, A. R., Qu, L., & Ruekert, R. W. (1999). Signaling unobservable product quality through a brand ally. *Journal of Marketing Research, 36*(2), 258–268.

Roth, M. S. (1994). Innovations in Defining and Measuring Brand Image. In *Advances in Consumer Research* , Chris T. Allen and Deborah Roedder John (Eds.). Provo, UT: Association for Consumer Research (Vol. 21), p. 495.

Rust, R. T. (2020). The future of marketing. *International Journal of Research in Marketing, 37*(1), 15–26.

Rust, R. T., Rand, W., Huang, M.-H., Stephen, A. T., Brooks, G., & Chabuk, T. (2021). Real-time brand reputation tracking using social media. *Journal of Marketing, 85*(4), 21–43.

Schaefer, M., & Rotte, M. (2007). Favorite brands as cultural objects modulate reward circuit. *NeuroReport, 18*(2), 141–145.

Shea, C. T., & Hawn, O. V. (2019). Microfoundations of corporate social responsibility and irresponsibility. *Academy of Management Journal, 62*, 1609–1642.

Simoes, C., Singh, J., & Perin, M. G. (2015). Corporate brand expressions in business-to-business companies' websites: Evidence from Brazil and India. *Industrial Marketing Management, 51*, 59–68.

Singh, J., Crisafulli, B., Quamina, L. T., & Kottasz, R. (2020b). The role of brand equity and crisis type on corporate brand alliances in crises. *European Management Review, 17*(4), 821–834.

Singh, J., Crisafulli, B., Quamina, L. T., & Xue, M. T. (2020a). 'To trust or not to trust': The impact of social media influencers on the reputation of corporate brands in crisis. *Journal of Business Research, 119*, 464–480.

Smith, A. K., Bolton, R. N., & Wagner, J. (1999). A model of customer satisfaction with service encounters involving failure and recovery. *Journal of Marketing Research, 36*(3), 356–372.

Valor, C., Antonetti, P., & Crisafulli, B. (2022). Emotions and consumers' adoption of innovations: An integrative review and research agenda. *Technological Forecasting & Social Change, 179*, 121609.

van Laer, T., Escalas, J. E., Ludwig, S., & van den Hende, E. A. (2019). What happens in Vegas stays on TripAdvisor? A theory and technique to understand narrativity in consumer reviews. *Journal of Consumer Research, 46*(2), 267–285.

Vargo, S. L., & Lusch, R. F. (2004). Evolving to a new dominant logic for marketing. *Journal of Marketing, 68*(1), 1–17.

Venkatraman, V., Dimoka, A., Pavlou, P. A. Et al. (2015). Predicting advertising success beyond traditional measures: New insights from neurophysiological methods and market response modeling. *Journal of Marketing Research, 52*(4), 436–452.

Verrastro, V., Fontanesi, L., Liga, F., Cuzzocrea, F., & Gugliandolo, M. C. (2020). Fear the Instagram: Beauty stereotypes, body image and Instagram use in a sample of male and female adolescents. *Qwerty Open and Interdisciplinary Journal of Technology, Culture and Education, 15*(1), 31–49.

Vrontis, D., Makrides, A., Christofi, M., & Thrassou, A. (2021). Social media influencer marketing: A systematic review, integrative framework and future research agenda. *International Journal of Consumer Studies, 45*(4), 1–28.

Wanjiru, E. (2005). Branding African countries: A prospect for the future. *Place Branding*, *2*(1), 84–95.

Wellman, M. L., Stoldt, R., Tully, M., & Ekdale, B. (2020). Ethics of authenticity: Social media influencers and the production of sponsored content. *Journal of Media Ethics*, *35*(2), 68–82.

Yoon, C., Gonzalez, R., Bechara, A., Berns, G. S., Dagher, A. A., Dubé, L., … Smidts, A. (2012). Decision neuroscience and consumer decision making. *Marketing Letters*, *23*(2), 473–485.

Yoon, C., Gonzales, R., & Bettman, J. R. (2009). Using fMRI to inform marketing research: Challenges and opportunities. *Journal of Marketing Research*, *46*(1), 17–19.

Yoon, C., Gutchess, A. H., Feinberg, F., & Polk, T. A. (2006). A functional magnetic resonance imaging study of neural dissociations between brand and person judgments. *Journal of Consumer Research*, *33*(1), 31–40.

Yurdakul, D., Atik, D., & Dholakia, N. (2017). Redefining the bottom of the pyramid from a marketing perspective. *Marketing Theory*, *17*(3), 289–303.

Index

Printed in the United States
by Baker & Taylor Publisher Services